Alternative Dispute Resolution

AUSTRALIA
The Law Book Company
Sydney

CANADA
The Carswell Company
Toronto, Ontario

INDIA
N.M. Tripathi Private Ltd.
Bombay
and
Eastern Law House Private Ltd.
Calcutta

M.P.P. House
Bangalore

Universal Book Traders
Delhi

ISRAEL
Steimatzky's Agency Ltd.
Tel Aviv

PAKISTAN
Pakistan Law House
Karachi

Alternative Dispute Resolution

*A Lawyer's Guide to Mediation and
other Forms of Dispute Resolution*

ALEXANDER H. BEVAN, M.A. (Oxon)
Solicitor

LONDON
SWEET & MAXWELL
1992

Published in 1992 by
Sweet & Maxwell Limited of
South Quay Plaza, 183 Marsh Wall
London, E14 9FT
Typeset by
Avonset, Midsomer Norton, Bath
Printed in Scotland

ISBN 0 421 47160 3

British Library Cataloguing in Publication Data

Bevan, Alexander H.
   Alternative dispute resolution: a lawyer's guide to
   mediation and other forms of dispute resolution.
   I. Title
   342.79

Foreword

'I know my rights' – through the ages the cry of the barrack-room lawyer: 'Know your rights' – through the land today the equally familiar cry of the media and the consumer lobby.

It is however a reflection of the schizophrenia of our age that as more and more people are aware of their rights, and as those rights themselves become more numerous, fewer and fewer people are able to enforce them.

I am not a lawer, but for more than a quarter of a century I have been closely involved with the law in action, as an insurer retaining lawyers for advice or litigation, as an 'expert' witness, and as director of a professional defence fund. Throughout that time I have been variously amused, enraged or driven to despair by the weaknesses, complexities and idiocies of 'the system'.

Even when litigation results in a just decision (not always the case, and even then not always visibly just in the perception of the parties), it rarely if ever provides complete recompense for the victorious party, and all too often the protagonists feel that they have been completely abandoned in a sea of incomprehensible legal, tactical and procedural complexities, in which their despairing cries are drowned, even if they are heard.

In fact, litigation at any level above the Small Claims Court is at best a Rolls-Royce affair; most of us have to travel in smaller, cheaper, less elaborate vehicles, but still we manage to complete our journeys safely and in reasonable comfort.

ADR, by contrast, offers speed, simplicity and the chance for all the parties
to play a major part in the resolution of the problem, in all except the smallest
cases at an affordable cost; if it also requires a willingness to compromise and to accept only 15oz of the despired pound of flesh, I believe that for most litigants, these are acceptable limitations.

It is not a cure for all the ills that commerce is heir to; but it does offer as good a chance of the right results as most litigation, and financially it is within the reach of most of us. Above all, it gives the parties the satisfaction of 'their day in court'; the chance to express their views, their frustrations, their sense of outrage or disappointment. True, it takes two to tango, and ADR requires two or more more or less reasonable opponents to make it work; but for the increasing proportion of this country's population unable to risk the uncertainties and financial reefs of litigation, it must be an increasingly acceptable alternative.

Mr Bevan has written a detailed, thoroughly researched, comprehensive and very readable guide. I have myself greatly benefited by reading it, and I hope that all its readers (of which there will be many), enjoy it as I did.

I am honoured by being given this opportunity of being associated with what I am confident will become a standard work on this new and exciting topic.

Charles Flaxman
Technical Director, Solicitors' Indemnity Fund Ltd
November 1991

Preface

My interest in mediation and alternative dispute resolution stems from my involvement in IDR Europe Ltd, which was started some three years ago and is Europe's first commercial mediation company. I would like to express my thanks to Bryan Beckett, Andrew Fraley, Richard Schiffer, Robert Wharton and Adrian Wheale, who in their different ways have all made a vital contribution to my knowledge and understanding of mediation.

I am very grateful to Andrew Floyer Acland, the author of *A Sudden Outbreak of Common Sense*, for his encouragement and guidance in writing this book. Needless to say, any errors are mine alone. A number of people have helped in the preparation of the book, including Nikki and Julie, and I thank them all too.

A.B.

Acknowledgments

The behaviour map in Chapter 6 is reproduced from *A Sudden Outbreak of Common Sense* by Andrew Floyer Acland (Hutchinson Business Books) by kind permission of the author and publisher.

The rules of arbitration prepared by US Arbitration and Mediation of Arizona, Nevada and New Mexico Inc. (Appendix 6) are reprinted by kind permission of that organisation.

Certain ADR contract clauses in Appendix 8 were drafted by Nigel Wildish of Turner Kenneth Brown, London and Roderick Charles I'Anson Banks, Barrister (the latter taken from *Lindley and Banks on Partnership*, published by Sweet & Maxwell) and are reprinted by kind permission of the respective authors and publishers.

The sample ADR clauses in Appendix 9 are copyright by the Center for Public Resources, New York and reprinted by permission.

Contents

List of Abbreviations

AAA   American Arbitration Association
ACAS   Advisory, Conciliation and Arbitration Service
ADR   Alternative dispute resolution
ADR Net   A group of law firms offering ADR services
          (see Appendix 7)
BAE   British Academy of Experts
BATNA   Best alternative to a negotiated agreement of Best alternative
          to no agreement (see Chapter 1 Part II)
CAC   Centre for Analysis of Conflict, University of Kent at
          Canterbury
CEDR   Centre for Dispute Resolution
CIArb   Chartered Institute of Arbitrators
CPR   Centre for Public Resources Inc. (New York)
E&O   Errors and omissions (insurance)
FIRM   Forum for Initiatives in Reparation and Mediation (now
          Mediation UK)
FMA   Family Mediators Association
IDR   International dispute resolution (IDR Europe Ltd)
LEADR   Lawyers Engaged in Alternative Dispute Resolution
          (Australia)
Med-arb   Mediation followed (if necessary) by arbitration (see Chapter
          1 Part II)
NEFF   Neutral expert fact-finding
NFCC   National Family Conciliation Council
SPIDR   Society for Professionals in Dispute Resolution
USA&M   United States Arbitration and Mediation Inc.
WOTNA   Worst outcome to no agreement

Relevant addresses are listed in Appendix 10

CHAPTER 1

Alternative Dispute Resolution

PART I – THE PHILOSOPHY OF ADR

'He leaned on a staggering lawyer.' – G. K. Chesterton

For a long time people have been worried about civil litigation. It is costly, time consuming, worrying and takes a long time to conclude. It is often thought to fall short of fairness. In part at least the Courts and Legal Services Act 1990 was aimed at improving civil justice. It follows on from other approaches to the system – the Report of the Civil Justice Review Body, Reviews of the Rules of the Supreme Court and a variety of changes over the years aimed at providing earlier disclosure of evidence, a 'cards on the table' approach and cheaper, more helpful and fairer justice. Courts are being designed to deal with specialised areas of work, developments in the Official Referees Court and the Commercial Court are examples. These changes must help. The situation is far better and the approach far more constructive than 50 years ago when, to cite an extreme example, a clerk issuing a writ could have it thrown back on the floor at him without explanation as to what the defect was – it might only have been a minor spelling mistake. In those days it seemed as if the court was also an adversary.

However, the underlying philosophy of the adversarial system remains that the parties using each piece of evidence, argument or point have to argue against each other, to prove their case before a judge who imposes a decision which usually leads to a win/lose result. Even if the case settles before trial, the mind-set or mental approach remains the same while the dispute lasts. The theory is that the truth of a dispute will surface through this adversarial process and thereby justice will be done.

The reality is that litigation does not always lead to a fair result and it is expensive in terms of time and money. The lack of fairness arises from various factors; poor, unspecialised or idiosyncratic judging can make the result a lottery depending on arbitrary points. If one party has a restricted purse, then the contest is immediately weighed against him. The richer party can pay for more skilled lawyers to exploit the intricacies of the system or simply hang on longer. Furthermore, even if the theory does work in practice and the truth does emerge, there is a high price or unpleasant side-effect in many cases: the system has led to the other side being *attacked* in a way which precludes future

1

co-operation, let alone business association. Finally, delay is exacerbated by the poor communication engendered in turn by the 'combat' mentality of litigation.

Alternative Dispute Resolution (ADR) is a term which refers to various procedures developed in the USA over the last 15 years or so in an attempt to overcome some of the weaknesses in the litigation and arbitration processes. The different ADR methods described below have in common the aims of blunting the adversarial attitude and encouraging more openness and better communication between the parties to a dispute. This leads to *earlier* settlement in appropriate cases with a saving in managerial and legal time, expense and worry. A by-product of ADR is that it is much more likely, where relevant, that the parties can continue to work together after the dispute has been terminated. Partnership disputes are a good example of this point. Whilst partners who have 'fallen out' may never again be full partners, there are many situations where a continuing relationship is necessary and where, therefore, ADR is more helpful than litigation.

The techniques of ADR can best be looked at in the context of each method. However, the general approach can be illustrated by the story of two cooks squabbling over an orange. The apocryphal judge selects an obscure reason for giving it to the first cook. The arbitrator divides it in half. The mediator asks each cook why they want it — to learn that one wants the peel for marmalade, the other the flesh for juice. The result is an optimisation of both parties' interests. The cooks and the mediator have looked at the problem from the point of view of interest rather than rights and positions, they have looked at the problem together.

ADR in the UK is new and attitudes towards it are not by any means fully developed. For any dispute to be appropriate for ADR there must be a basic willingness on both sides to give the process a try, rather than cynically to exploit the trust that ADR relies upon. The aim of this book is to expand knowledge of the subject and how it works, in order to foster more positive attitudes towards it. The target or pitch of the book is the legal profession, because most formal dispute resolution will continue to involve lawyers. ADR will not supersede litigation, which for some cases will remain the only appropriate resolution method and for other cases will still be a powerful option. Thus, lawyers will play a vital role in choosing whether to use ADR and at what stage.

Equally, ADR will provide a useful addition to the litigation tool-kit. The advent of ADR is to be looked at by the lawyer not as a threat but as an opportunity — a way to lighten his and his client's load.

PART II – THE DIFFERENT ADR PROCEDURES

'Man propounds negotiating, man accepts the compromise. Very rarely will he squarely push the logic of a fact to its ultimate conclusion in unmitigated act.' – Rudyard Kipling, *The Female of the Species*

Negotiation

A lot of disputes end after the parties negotiate a settlement themselves. Negotiation, therefore, is a basic dispute-resolution process. This is true both as to conflict outside the legal system and as to conflicts which reach the hands of lawyers. Negotiation forms an important part of everyday life and an important part of *all* lawyers' work. It is perhaps surprising that there is still little formal negotiation training yet available for lawyers and even the toughest lawyer-negotiators are largely self-taught. That gap is beginning to be filled and negotiation training courses are now available.

A detailed analysis of negotiation is well beyond the scope of this book but it is both a subject in its own right and a key part of most non-adjudicatory dispute resolution methods; accordingly, I will deal with some of its aspects.

Approaches to Negotiation
There are a number of approaches to negotiation and similarly a variety of types of negotiator. Roger Fisher and William Ury of Harvard University in *Getting to Yes* advocate what they described as **principled negotiation**. They suggest that, in contrast to haggling or bartering, an objective approach, deciding issues on their merits is (a) more acceptable and (b) more likely to achieve a mutually advantageous result. Key elements of their approach are:

(1) *Separating people from the problem*; in other words attacking the problem, not each other.

(2) *Focusing on interests, not positions*; this involves a deeper analysis of the reasons for a dispute and, it is argued, can lead to common interests being revealed.

(3) *Insisting on objective criteria*; this arises because not all bargaining can result in a 'win-win' outcome. Risk of negotiating failure can be lessened by the parties agreeing, for example, on objective methods of resolution – rather than lose trade over the price of a second-hand car, parties can agree to apply the relevant figures from *Glass's Guide*.

Know your best alternative to a negotiated agreement (BATNA)
Only by accurately assessing what results you could obtain in the absence of agreement can you properly decide whether or not to enter into a negotiated agreement. Using the second-hand car case, it is always necessary to find out what *other* similar cars actually cost before negotiating on a particular vehicle. The BATNA can change; during negotiations information might be revealed which increases or decreases the BATNA. It is an important part of negotiation technique to be conscious of where the BATNA stands at any particular moment. This applies to your own case and the other side's. In some instances it is possible to alter your opponent's BATNA. In union negotiation an extreme example is for the management to say, 'If you don't do a deal we shall make 200 people redundant.'

Another view of negotiation is that, ultimately, it is **power-centred**. Not every dispute can be resolved by recognising compatible interests and crafting the right solution. Sometimes one party can only gain at the expense of the other. This 'zero-sum' or 'distributive' bargaining situation may be partially amenable to principled negotiation but in the end bargaining power will prevail and a contest of wills cannot be avoided.

This begs the question, what is bargaining power? There are a number of types of negotiating power. Straightforward financial or economic power is easily recognised. There is also the power of skill and knowledge, of existing relationships, of a good alternative to negotiation and what Fisher calls the power of commitment. This power of commitment operates on the basis that if one party to a negotiation commits himself 'irrevocably' to a figure or stance, then, so long as the figure or stance is within the negotiation range of the other side and he does not adopt an even more rigid position, that will be the result of the negotiation. This is because the other side considers he is at risk of losing a deal that is better than his walk-away position. Let us say I am the plaintiff's lawyer in a personal injury action hoping for £45,000 damages but willing to accept £35,000. I may face an insurer hoping to get away with £30,000 but prepared to go to £40,000. The range within which both of us would be better off settling than walking away is between £35,000 and £40,000. If I can convince the insurer that counsel has advised £40,000 and the client knows this and will not accept 'a penny less', then I am invoking the power of commitment and may succeed in getting £40,000. An extreme example of this is the case of the lorry driver who, facing an oncoming lorry with room for one vehicle only, conspicuously throws away his steering wheel. Seeing this, the other driver will save his life by giving way.

The tendency is for mediators to encourage parties to adopt principled nego-tiation, but it would be naive to expect power to play no part in the resolution of a dispute and it is useful to analyse what types of power are being applied, in order to decide how to use or, alternatively, resist them. It is also useful to analyse what type of negotiator you naturally are, hard-line or interest-based; competitive or co-operative. Research in America, based upon the perceptions of practising lawyers about their fellow attorneys, suggests that both types of negotiator can be very effective but there are a lot more co-operative negotiators.

Competitives place a higher emphasis on getting a good result for their client than on ethical behaviour. Co-operatives place ethical behaviour above other considerations. Whichever type you are may depend less on choice than personality and character. On the other hand, a degree of versatility and the ability to change roles can enhance negotiating performance.

The process
Whatever type of negotiator you are, there must be thorough preparation and careful assessment of the different issues. The presentation involves knowing

your own case, your opponent's case, how the process will develop, what conventions will apply, where they will take place and who should make the opening offer.

Knowing your own case involves a careful assessment of your BATNA (best alternative to a negotiated agreement) in order that you can work out your bottom line – the absolute minimum you would be prepared to settle for. Your BATNA in a legal dispute will involve an assessment of the likelihood of success as well as the value you put on your claim. It will also be necessary to assess your worst outcome to no agreement (WOTNA), to enable you to test the reasonableness and realism of your bottom line or reserve price. Then collect your arguments and facts/evidence in support.

A similar approach is applied to your opponent's case. Consider his BATNA and WOTNA and what the strengths and weaknesses of his case are. How has he conducted negotiations in the past and what is his reputation? What arguments can you use to encourage him to re-assess his BATNA? An example of this occurred when I was negotiating for a client in a dispute involving considerable delay by a sub-contractor. The aim of both parties was to agree terms for the delayed work to be re-done and to agree some compensation. By stressing that my client had the legal option to go elsewhere and claim the difference in price (which would have been substantial), I reminded the other side that their BATNA was not simply a matter of a court's view of the terms for re-doing the work and compensation for delay.

The next step is the opening offer. If you decide to go first, consider the advantages of an extreme opening offer;

(1) It anchors the negotiations at your preferred level; particularly if the other side are ill prepared they may begin to think their bottom line is unrealistic.

(2) It enhances the prospects of the final result being higher, since there is a tendency for negotiations to end somewhere close to the mid-point of two opening positions.

(3) The strategy of opening at a reasonable figure and sticking fast can irritate the other side, who have to make all the concessions.

However there are also disadvantages to extreme offers:

(1) It can disrupt and even destroy the process.

(2) An unrealistic offer can lead to having to make large concessions which weaken credibility.

(3) In any event the other side may think you are stupid for being so wide of the mark. They would then be wisest to counter with a lower figure than get anchored to haggling at your level.

The negotiation now commences. A common pattern is for the concessions to become smaller as the meeting progresses, and the interval between concessions also becomes smaller. The suggestion to the other side is that you are reaching your limit. They are probably playing a similar game. How far you go depends upon such things as your confidence in fighting the case in court, how important it is to settle rather than make some 'profit' in the sense of bettering your bottom line and how prepared you and your client are to dissemble. Concealing your true position can involve a trade-off between professional integrity and optimising the result of the negotiation.

Is it right and ethical to say 'I am unable to take away less than £x,000' when in reality you have authority to go to a lower figure? Ethics and self-interest can co-incide in this situation in that if you really think a lower position will be necessary, too strong a commitment makes your later concession seem like weakness, undermining your credibility.

There is some debate in America about the ethics of telling lies (white or black) in the negotiations. Some argue that negotiations are the legal equivalent of poker playing or the bargaining of a market-place. Therefore, some tolerance of dishonesty is both necessary and realistic. Others (Professor Ruth Fleet Thurman, Professor of Law, Stetson University College of Law, among them) argue that lawyers must aspire to the highest ethical standards. Anything less than complete honesty runs counter to the need for high self-acceptance. It undermines the profession and leads to imitation and retaliation.

At the end of the day, settlement may not be achievable, regardless of ethics. A break of a few weeks can lead to objective changes in the situation and subjective changes in both parties' assessment of it. A technique which is useful in most ADR processes and in deadlocked negotiation, is to help your opponent off his hook. In other words, to help save his face or to find a further range of common interests, to allow trade-offs and movement. Getting him off the hook can be difficult face to face, since what may well be your enlightened self-interest can be misinterpreted as weakness or cynicism. Hence the development of ADR processes and the introduction of third party neutrals.

In this country the usual progression from failed negotiation is to litigation or arbitration. Now this is no longer the only option available to the lawyer and the client.

ADR processes

'Discourage litigation, persuade your neighbours to compromise whenever you can. Point out to them how the nominal winner is often a loser in fees, expenses and cost of time.' — Abraham Lincoln.

Having taken a quick look at traditional settlement negotiation, we must now consider what are the different types of ADR process. The following list is not comprehensive but covers those most commonly used.

Some elements of binding decision making

Arbitration	Med-arb
Adjudication	Rent-a-judge/Private judging

Non-binding
Mediation
Conciliation (often confused with mediation)
Family mediation
Mini-trials
Ombudsmen
Neutral expert fact-finding
Summary jury trials

Binding processes: Arbitration

Despite being procedurally less formal than litigation and being private (until litigated), arbitration is most like litigation and can be something of a misfit within ADR. It is binding and basically adversarial and has been around for hundreds of years.

Theoretical positive aspects of arbitration are:
- The ability to select a decision maker with appropriate expertise for the dispute
- Procedural informality
- Privacy and therefore, to a degree, confidentiality
- Speed and therefore lower cost
- Finality of decision

Arbitration arises either by virtue of clauses in contracts or terms of collective agreements or 'voluntarily' once conflict has developed. Its longevity suggests that in practice as well as theory it has merits. It is widely used in international trade disputes. Although most of the above advantages are in contrast to litigation, it must be said that its 'finality' gives it an edge over other less 'intrusive' ADR methods in the eyes of some critics of ADR. These people argue that the proponents of alternative dispute resolution overstate their case, that either the pressures of non-binding methods lead to unfair agreement or the process does no more than what would have happened anyway, and the finality of arbitration gives it a rigour which is absent elsewhere.

A reasonable, though sweeping view of these matters seems to be that arbitration certainly has its place but that it has lost some of its shine and glamour. Being a process requiring parties to present evidence and arguments in a comprehensive way, it can be long and expensive. My experience is that it is not currently popular in the sense that people do not speak fondly of it. It is, for example, compared unfavourably with litigation for its lack of vigour – including the lack of court mandate during the interlocutory stages and for the very finality raised above.

Appeals from an arbitrator's decision are severely limited – currently to questions of procedural fairness and the arbitrator's conduct. On the other hand it is compared unfavourably with, say, mediation because the arbitrator is not able to uncover the 'private agenda', the interests of the parties rather than their positions. This is because, however sympathetic the arbitrator is and informal the procedure, the parties know that a binding decision has to be made and are therefore less willing to disclose their full hand, strengths and weaknesses.

Recently in America a number of states and federal districts have developed compulsory but non-binding arbitration schemes, as a necessary preliminary to litigation. A hybrid of mediation and arbitration is med-arb which I shall discuss below. The ADR movement itself has therefore embraced the idea of arbitration and it may be that the more traditional forms of arbitration will benefit from ADR ideas about communication and moderating the adversarial nature of traditional dispute resolution.

I recently attended an arbitration in Phoenix, Arizona, carried out in the offices of a US Attorney, Bryce Buehler, active in providing ADR services. This was a claim by a couple for damages of about £15,000 ($30,000) arising out of a car accident and alleged whiplash injuries. The defence insurers were unwilling to settle, believing that the claim was manufactured against their indemnified, an elderly lady driving a Lincoln car. This case was therefore not appropriate for mediation but could have been expensive to litigate. The costs of the arbitration, which lasted 3½ hours and needed another 1½ hours of the arbitrator's time to give a reasoned reserved judgment, were about £600. This actually compares favourably with a trial in the UK, since there would be barrister's fees, witness expenses and so forth. This arbitration dispensed with the right of appeal and although it followed the procedural pattern of a trial with examination and cross-examination, it was much swifter and less formal (and intimidating) than a trial. The parties also had the option, not exercised, to put a floor and roof on the arbitrator's award.

There seems to be no reason why there should not be an introduction of arbitration of this type into the UK. The success of the transplantation will depend upon a body of fair and competent practitioners coming forward and there will be a need for solicitors to have the courage of their convictions to prosecute the cases themselves. It should also be noted that the American system of deposition-taking means that the case there is well-prepared. There is a risk that cases here would be unready with a consequent waste of time and money.

Med-Arb

Mr Justice Phillips, in a Channel 4 television programme on the legal system shown in late 1988, put it graphically when he said he often wanted to bang the parties' heads together in cases where he couldn't see why they continued to fight. Some judges do take part in alternative dispute resolution during their cases. They ask questions designed not only to elicit legal argument, but also to uncover the real issues. They drop broad hints as to how, given 'hypothetical' findings, they might decide this or that matter. They try to encourage the parties towards a realistic approach, but they can only go so far and retain judicial propriety. Similarly, some arbitrators become involved in possible settlement attempts before a decision is imposed.

Med-arb has developed in America to allow, with the consent of the parties, for the same person to both mediate and, if that is unsuccessful, then arbitrate a dispute. The trouble, it is argued, is that the third-party neutral selected muddies the adjudicative waters by delving into mediation and learning about matters which are irrelevant and prejudicial to the decision-making function. So far as I am aware med-arb has not been practised in this country, so a hypothetical illustration of this problem might go as follows: An arbitrator uses mediation initially in a dispute over commercial rent. While discovering about the strengths and weaknesses of the tenant's case he learns that the tenant plans to sub-let to a company that has already agreed a rental value above the landlord's opening position. This might be a matter quite outside the scope of the arbitration as set out in the lease, but must surely influence the arbitrator in favour of a higher rent.

Various suggestions have been made to improve the position. One is for there to be an arbitrator appointed by each party with a neutral chairman arbitrator in the middle; this is called tripartite arbitration. The format of industrial tribunals in this country is similar, with a wing member from the employer and the employee sides of industry sitting with a lawyer chairman. Industrial tribunals are still basically adversarial in form, however, and the wing members have no 'brief' for one or other side other than perhaps a background sympathy. In tripartite arbitration the role of the wing members is much trickier and the phrase 'being all things to all men' springs to mind. Wing members can neither be full-time advocates of their 'clients' nor impartial judges, since they learn confidential information and one of their functions is to represent a point of view.

Another variant is for the wing members to have no decision-making role. This takes away one of the perceived advantages of med-arb, namely that the mediator has a powerful weapon – his power to *decide* at the end of the process – in order to encourage parties to adopt a realistic approach to the case. He is then little more than an advocate sitting in on the adjudication.

A further variant is for the arbitrator to act first as a mediator and then as *advisory* arbitrator. The neutral party here has no power to decide but he does have the right to advise as to the likely outcome if the case does go on to full arbitration. An extension of this is for the advisory arbitrator to be able to recommend a course of action to the 'tribunal' that will ultimately decide in the event of the med-arb failing. This has been tried in child custody cases in California and raises questions about the extent to which a mediator can be asked in court about what he has learned during the mediation. The trouble is that whether the mediator/arbitrator decides or simply recommends, his dual role has a significant impact on the way in which the parties approach the mediation phase of the process. In short, his decision or advice role will impair his ability to draw the parties away from the confrontational and towards a joint problem-solving approach that is fundamental to ADR.

The above discussion raises important issues for ADR, and ADR practitioners, which I will touch on again under mediation. For the moment, I draw the tentative conclusion that med-arb is an interesting idea but fraught with difficulty. This is particularly so when the parties are unwilling, or at best sceptical, participants in ADR. Their natural inclination in case of doubt will be to fall back on point-scoring traditional methods of case presentation. On the other hand, if both the parties need and want to settle their case and genuinely see the merits of ADR, then the problems of med-arb can be overcome.

It is argued by some that the ADR movement is naive in thinking that distributive bargaining or zero-sum disputes ('one for me is one less for you') can be solved with a win/win result. Objectively, one party has to do worse than the other in many cases; but on the other hand, a settlement at an early stage can be a good result for both parties. I think med-arb is best looked at as an extension of mediation rather than arbitration. If a case needs to be *decided*, probably largely because the parties do not have the right attitude, then arbitration or litigation is the right course and med-arb is no substitute. If however, the parties do have the necessary trust in ADR but the settlement process needs some muscle, perhaps because of some large differences, then some form of med-arb is valuable.

In several mediations I have done, I have felt the wish and willingness of both parties to settle but an inability by one side to accept, on a key issue, that a decision of a court could go against him. In an ideal world I would have plucked out of the ether a perfectly qualified arbitrator to decide that issue, leaving me to get on with the assisted negotiation once that hurdle had been passed. It is interesting that in September 1990 the London Common Law and Commercial Bar Association put forward a proposal, later endorsed by the Lord Chancellor, for a voluntary court-annexed ADR scheme. It involves basic mediation with the conciliator passing from side to side, discussing the merits of each party's case, but if agreement cannot be achieved the conciliator gives his assessment of the likely result of a trial. Using the 'Calderbank' idea, they hint that if a party does significantly worse than the assessment at trial, then there could be a costs implication. This is a recommendation to the Bar Council, but could develop into a practical example of med-arb.

Adjudication

This term is often used in ADR literature as one of the primary dispute-resolution processes in contrast to arbitration, negotiation and mediation. In this sense it is dispute-resolution by litigation and it takes place in the High Court, County Court and various Tribunals. Confusingly, arbitrators also adjudicate.

Adjudication is also a specific form of alternative dispute resolution in the notoriously dispute-ridden construction industry. The idea is to bring about a quick end to the dispute, to allow the contract to complete. If at the end of the works, one or both parties are dissatisfied with the adjudicator's decision, they can then refer the matter to an arbitrator who is not bound by the earlier 'decision'.

Adjudication therefore has in common with other forms of ADR the aim of speedy resolution. It also shows the move away from the adversarial system, inasmuch as the adjudicator inquires into the matter, by obtaining statements and documents, by way of investigating rather than deciding after the parties have contested the matter before a quasi-judicial forum. It is of note that he is an expert, and not an arbitrator, in most forms of adjudication clause. Such clauses can be found in the JCT Design and Build Contract and the HCT Form of Sub-Contract. Here is a procedure which also combines non-adversarial problem-solving with an imposed decision. The emphasis is rather more on decision than consensus, since the adjudicator has, above all, a job to do – to get the project started again. It may be that over time adjudication will borrow more from mediation, since it is a substantial bonus if the decision sticks after hand-over of the works.

Rent-a-judge/private judging

This involves the parties selecting an acceptable judge, often a retired judge, to decide the case privately. He is paid by the parties and once his decision has been imposed it is enforceable as if it had been given by a court. Furthermore, it is appealable (unlike an arbitrator's decision) on grounds of law or that it is against the weight of the evidence.

The system operates in California under the Californian Reference Statute, in other words a case is referred by the court. To operate it here would undoubtedly involve a change in the Rules of the Supreme Court, and probably fresh legislation. Accordingly, I will not dwell too long on the subject. It is interesting to note that an ADR body known as 'JAMS' has developed in California consisting of retired judges and is making headway in this field as well as mediation and arbitration.

The advantages and disadvantages of the system do nevertheless highlight aspects of the litigation-ADR debate. For instance, an important attraction is the ability to select the right person to judge the case. This is often cited as one of the lotteries and disadvantages of litigation. It could also be that having selected the judge, neither party is as keen to appeal, another perceived disadvantage of litigation over arbitration.

Other advantages are speed, convenience, flexibility and confidentiality, although the secrecy of the process is also a source of criticism. Public justice is not simply the prerogative of the criminal and if rent-a-judge aims to parallel the court system, but without its negative aspects, perhaps it ought, too, to be subject to public scrutiny.

A major criticism is cost. It is called 'rich man's justice'. The fear is that if the concept took off, then powerful business and commercial interests would take their cases out of the public civil justice system with resultant under-funding and second-class status of the residue. This is unlikely to occur in practice, since even to take a case to rent-a-judge requires agreement on referral which is often too high a hurdle for parties locked in combative litigation.

Perhaps a more cogent criticism is that unlike mini-trials, this process does not encourage a movement away from adversarial attitudes and is even more adversarial than arbitration.

It remains to be seen whether the idea has any future over here, but it is an amusing prospect to have ex-Law Lords travelling the country in large container lorries kitted out as court rooms, dispensing private justice. In the current mood of attack on the judiciary, the impetus for these developments may not come from the litigants alone. Some judges may be looking for work.

Non-binding Processes

Recent developments in the UK have led to two major forms of ADR coming to the fore, mini-trials and mediation. I propose to deal with mini-trials and an assortment of minor forms of non-binding ADR in this chapter and then devote the balance of the book to mediation, about which I have the most direct experience.

Mini-Trials

This is not just another form of private judging or quasi-trial. It is a method of resolving disputes, primarily business disputes, that uses techniques of negotiation, mediation and advisory arbitration.

There are a number of variants used in the United States but the basic programme is as follows:

(1) The parties agree, often through a commercial or public organisation such as the Centre for Public Resources in the USA or CEDR in the UK, to conduct a mini-trial. In this country CEDR (the Centre for Dispute Resolution) is the main provider.

(2) Having agreed to the process and what rules will apply, the parties exchange important documents, witness and expert statements, and intro-ductory addresses in a form of core discovery. If the process does not succeed,

fuller discovery can be dealt with in the resumed commercial litigation. This is the information exchange phase.

(3) A neutral adviser is jointly selected by the parties. He has no power to bind the parties but uses mediation techniques, and at the end may be asked to give a view as to the likely outcome if the case has to go to trial. During the mini-trial he can, if he has appropriate expertise, be asked to give opinions on parts of the law and evidence. It is for this reason that neutrals are often ex-judges or figures of some standing in the legal world; alternatively, they are specialists in the subject-matter of the dispute.

(4) The parties and their lawyers convene at a suitable place with high-level executives or representatives for each side. These are people to whom the case is presented and who later seek to negotiate a settlement. They have two important characteristics. First, they are people who have not been directly involved in the dispute as it has built up within their organisation and therefore they have less of a vested interest in an outright win to save face. Secondly, they must have authority to settle the case or at least be very influential in the decision-making processes of their company. It is preferable if they have authority to settle on the day.

(5) At the mini-trial the lawyers make truncated presentations of their case. The aim is to be concise rather than comprehensive and the experience from abroad is that each presentation lasts between one and six hours and the mini-trial from between half a day to three or four days, depending on complexity. Sometimes the presentation is by lawyers alone, sometimes witnesses are called, and experts also. There are no formal rules of evidence and the aim is to get at the strengths and weaknesses of each side's case as quickly as possible and to give the executives the flavour of what a full-blown trial might be like. The difference is the informality which can, for instance, allow the executives to ask questions and even break off for negotiations before the formal presentations are complete. Another common feature is the open question and answer session when anyone can put questions to anyone else.

(6) The neutral adviser is usually only called for an opinion if the post-presentation negotiations have broken down. The value of this is to enable the parties to re-assess their BATNAS (see page 3) and hopefully re-convene settlement discussions. If there is still no result, then, usually, the parties are free to continue with the appropriate form of dispute resolution (usually litigation) on the basis that the the mini-trial has been confidential and without prejudice and the neutral is not available for advice or to give evidence in subsequent proceedings.

The process is flexible in design and sometimes an expert in the subject-matter of the dispute is selected; sometimes the neutral is simply a mediator who facilitates the process but has no capacity to give legal opinions or give authoritative evidence as to the likely trial result. The nature and qualities of a suitable neutral can be of great importance to the process and training and selection are matters which will need careful attention as mini-trials and ADR become more common.

A London-based organisation, the Centre for Dispute Resolution (CEDR), has gathered together a panel of suitable neutrals, having trained them with the assistance of experienced American practitioners. CEDR itself is set up on the lines of the Centre for Public Resources in the United States, with participants from leading legal and accountancy firms, industry and commerce all pledging to use ADR before litigating with each other; as such it is non-profit making. My own company, IDR (Europe) Ltd (IDR), dealing primarily with mediation, also has extensive training facilities covering the basic techniques of ADR, in particular mediation and negotiation. IDR has a panel of trained mediators who may be appropriate mini-trial neutrals, particularly if the variant selected does not involve a 'quasi-decision'. This panel of mediators comes largely from practising lawyers within ADR Net Ltd, a non-profit making association of large firms of solicitors formed to promote the ideas of ADR and its use in this country.

An early example of a US mini-trial took place in the late 1970s. It concerned an intellectual property dispute between a company holding rights over credit-rating computer devices used by department stores and a company alleged to have infringed the patents. Litigation was commenced and huge amounts of discovery ensued. It was decided to speed up the process by limiting the information exchange to a short period and then conducting negotiations with a neutral adviser (an ex-judge) and chief executive officers (CEOs) from each company present. Eventually, a solution and settlement was achieved which included a variety of commercial features that could not have been ordered by a judge. A future relationship was nurtured.

What then determines whether a dispute is suitable for this form of ADR?

First, the type of dispute will be important. Experience in the United States suggests that cases involving mixed fact and law are more suitable than these which are either all legal or all fact-based. If the parties agree the facts but the law is in issue the courts can be quite quick and they are still probably the best forum for resolution. If the facts are central to a dispute, then there is a good chance that the credibility of one or more of the witnesses is a key factor and therefore the informality of the mini-trial may not be ideal to really test the evidence. Cases involving substantial expert evidence can be suitable because extreme views held by experts can be modified in the 'realistic' atmosphere of the mini-trial and even if agreement is not reached, the issue may have been narrowed and clarified to the extent that the trial is brought closer and will last less time.

Secondly, and even more importantly, the attitude and relationship of the parties will determine whether a mini-trial is possible and desirable. It is a common thread running throughout ADR that the attitude and 'mind-set' of the parties is vital to its success. There are very few cases that are unsuitable if both sides really want to settle; wardship might be an example since the court's jurisdiction cannot be ousted. Equally, however objectively suitable a case might be, if one side is taking a negative stance or cynically seeking to exploit the process, then the mini-trial is likely to be inappropriate and fail. Likely, because it could just be that one person from the truculent side, be it a lawyer or executive, is prepared to take an open view and try to make the thing work. But if, say, one side has more to gain by delay or there are other technical reasons for litigation, then ADR is inappropriate. The relationship of the parties is important. If they wish to continue to do business with each other, and in other respects the process is suitable, then, as with mediation, mini-trials enhance the prospect of preserving and continuing the association.

It is likely that mini-trials will mainly be used for large-value commercial cases since they are more expensive than most other forms of ADR, save perhaps arbitration. This is because although the process is flexible, it is nevertheless more formal and takes more organisation than mediation. Even the prior agreement over which rules to apply and what format to use can take time and is therefore expensive.

Conciliation

This is a term that has led to some confusion. Some people, notably those in the building industry, see conciliation as what I shall later describe as mediation, with the conciliator (a) imposing no decision and (b) not even giving an opinion. Others, and I refer to the London Common Law and Commercial Bar Association Pilot Scheme proposal, see conciliation as being distinct from mediation in that the conciliator *does*, ultimately, give an opinion and an assessment as to the likely trial outcome.

The terms mediation and conciliation are basically interchangeable, but it is partly because conciliation already has connotations of industrial relations and family matters that I shall use the term 'mediation' for the process of a neutral party acting as go-between assisting communication and hopefully, negotiating between parties in conflict. The other reason for using the term is that this is the name given to the process in the United States and my company IDR (Europe) Limited has developed and marketed it in the United Kingdom with that name. IDR talks about 'commercial mediation' to distinguish it from family mediation, although commercial is used in its widest sense and includes personal injury disputes, partnership disputes and many other contests as well as disputes which, if they go to court, are known as 'commercial litigation'.

Dr Karl Mackie, Chief Executive of CEDR and a leading proponent of ADR, usefully talks about 'facilitative' and 'evaluative' mediation. Facilitative mediation is at one end of the spectrum; the mediator does not express an opinion and is primarily a catalyst to enable the parties to communicate better: he introduces an important element of objectivity. At the other end of the spectrum is evaluative mediation where the neutral persuades the parties to settle by giving opinions on law, facts and evidence. There is no reason why these approaches should not mingle and sometimes evaluative mediation can take place first.

Family mediation

This has been practised in England and Wales for some years now and is therefore the first active ADR process to take root here (excluding arbitration).

The usual format is for there to be two mediators, one a practising matrimonial lawyer, the other a probation officer. The mediation takes place with all the parties present all the time, which distinguishes it from commercial mediation, of which a key element is the separating of the parties and the holding of private sessions or 'caucuses' when the mediator learns in confidence about the 'private agendas' of each side. The reason for the difference is that there is a very real fear that to go off into private meetings would weaken the all-important trust that a family mediator must develop with husband and wife. The party left alone might start imagining bias on the part of the absent mediator.

It is because of the delicate nature of divorce and family disputes and the emotional aspect of most such cases, with the risk of coercion, or at least manipulation, that the checks and balances of a court-based resolution system are probably still needed to run alongside family mediation. Thus, for example, a consent order may still need court approval, whereas a negotiated settlement in the 'commercial' field rarely needs to undergo any court scrutiny. Issues are raised here well beyond the scope of this book and there are other alternatives to court-imposed decisions that operate in the family field. At the moment this solution is not available to all couples since legal aid is not granted for mediation and the cost of the mediators takes it out of the range of most people falling within (and outside) the financial criteria for legal aid eligibility.

Summary jury trials and expert neutral fact-finding

These are two developments mentioned to illustrate the way dispute resolution can adapt. The first has little or no application in this country. The second may well have.

In America, civil trials often involve a jury and the idea behind the summary jury trial is to allow the parties and their lawyers to see how a mock jury will deal with the case after a truncated presentation of the legal case to them. Lawyers can question the jury about their verdict and how they came to it. It seems that the process works quite well, although academically sound statistics are difficult to come by. It is interesting that there seems to be quite a lot of lawyer support for the idea as being better and giving more impetus to settle than many other pre-trial proceedings. In this country the prevailing view of the judiciary and the legal establishment is that pre-trial hearings are a waste of time. Might it not be worthwhile designing more imaginative processes as part of the litigation system which get the parties thinking earlier about the broad issues of the case and stimulate settlement discussions? In Florida there is a court-imposed mediation scheme with a different judge vetting cases to see if they are suitable for ADR. Such a system could work here, especially if the parties knew the process would be confidential and the judge would not try the case subsequently.

Neutral expert fact-finding (NEFF) is based on the problem that arises in complex technical cases, when each side has an expert holding firmly to a view that is diametrically opposed to that of the opponent's expert. NEFF can arise either through appointment by the court (in the United States) of a neutral expert or by agreement between the parties.

It is a well known feature of litigation that experts can be more partisan than the clients themselves. The idea behind NEFF is for the neutral to re-evaluate the technical evidence and encourage the parties to look critically at their own expert's assessment. In some cases it is the expert's view that is the main plank in a party's assessment of its chances of success and hence its attitude towards settlement. A revision in the expert's view can lead to agreement.

I recently dealt with a mediation case involving quite complex technical arguments in a construction industry dispute. The aim of the mediation was to get each side to appreciate the strengths and weaknesses of its case in order to get negotiations started within the possible range of negotiation options. It was not until one side's expert adjusted his view and conceded that there was an area of vulnerability in one aspect of the technical case that the bargaining got started. The trouble is that neutral experts don't appear to be much loved. The parties question the need to pay yet another expert. The lawyers are concerned at too open a discussion with someone whose opinion might tellingly go against the case. The experts resent an intruder and, it is said in America, the judge resents the fact that there is another genuine neutral in court to compete with.

Neutral experts are in a lonely position since their only power in the settlement process is to criticise and weaken the testimony of one or both of the fellow experts, a negative power that doesn't endear them to anyone save perhaps the party who thinks he is getting a good deal. However, whilst it may take some time for the notion to develop as a procedure in its own right, in both mini-trials and some mediations (and of course arbitration) the idea of an independent expert influencing the outcome is not novel and in some circumstances is fundamental to the process.

CHAPTER 2

Mediation

Mediation is the use of a third party to help those in conflict to do things and reach agreements which, unaided, they may never do, or may do so much later in the conflict that each side will have suffered further harm. The idea is to assist people to talk to each other in a rational and problem-solving way, to clear up misunderstandings and clarify issues and to help negotiations by bringing realism and objectivity to a dispute. Above all, the process aims to put back in the hands of the parties responsibility for the outcome. A judge or arbitrator makes a decision which closes the contest in litigation and arbitration; in a successful mediation the contestants themselves decide on the outcome.

How the process works

Once all parties to a dispute, which may well already be litigation, have agreed to mediate, then a location and time are arranged and a mediator selected. It is usual for the parties attending to send representatives who have full authority to settle the case. Lawyers are also encouraged to attend, both to assist in presentation and legal argument and, if agreement is reached, to draw up settlements that are binding in law.

The mediation begins with a joint session and everyone present. The mediator makes an opening statement explaining what mediation is and what the mediator's role is — he asks each side in turn to address him with a presentation of the case and their position. Typically, these opening statements, which may be in writing, should last no more than ten to fifteen minutes, even in complex matters. There is then an opportunity to ask questions, both of the mediator and the other side. At this point the joint session is adjourned and the mediator sees each side privately, in what the Americans call 'caucus', more elegantly termed private session in England and Wales.

To return to the mediator's opening statement, it is important for this to put the parties at ease and to emphasise that the mediator is there to help and guide but not to force anyone or anything. He must square the circle and create an 'inoffensive presence'. I will deal now with the words that might be used in such an opening statement:

(1) 'My name is Alex Bevan, I am the mediator today and I believe both sides have been given details of my background.

(2) May I ask you to introduce yourselves, going from left to right.

(3) Thank you for coming here today, the aim is to achieve an acceptable agreement and my task is to help you do this.

(4) The procedure is straightforward: at the end of my address I will ask each party, in turn, to make an *opening statement* setting out their understanding of the case but without engaging in settlement discussions at this stage, i.e. no negotiating figures yet. Then I will see the plaintiff in *private session* and afterwards, likewise, the defendant. Finally, we will have a *closing session* to discuss, I hope, an agreement.

(5) Mediation is:

Voluntary – You can leave when you want, but I hope you will stay to try it out.

Non-binding – I do not, and cannot, impose a decision.

Without prejudice – If a binding agreement is reached, then this would no longer apply.

Confidential – The whole session is confidential but private sessions are too, and I will only release to the other side what is permitted save in respect of information which is already in the public domain.

(6) The *mediation* is chaired by me. My role is to *guide the discussion*, clarify issues and help both sides to a *clearer understanding of their strengths and weaknesses*. I am not a judge and there are *no rules of evidence*. An important technique I will use is to be the *devil's advocate* and ask what I hope will be tough questions. I will do this to both sides – don't take personal offence.

(7) If we can reach agreement, then it is put in writing and signed. Thank you for participating. Do you have any questions?'

This is a little truncated and different mediators will add individual flavour, but I think it contains the key elements of mediation.

It should be recognised that this inoffensive presence can only in part be learned; to some extent the mediator must have the right personality – a true ability to listen and empathise, allied to a firmness and clarity of thought that matches, and preferably overreaches, those of others present.

It is the private session or caucus that is the engine room of the process, the stage that develops the movement which hopefully, turns into rapid negotiation and in many cases, settlement.

The private sessions usually commence with the mediator seeing the claimant or plaintiff. He then sees the defendant or respondent. If there are more than two parties then each will be seen alone but grouping may well develop later, enabling the mediator to limit the number of different sessions he has to conduct. There may be three or more rounds of caucusing before the joint session is re-convened, either to check settlement terms or to acknowledge that the parties have gone as far as they are able on the day.

What goes on in these private sessions? I shall attempt to explain in some detail below. I say attempt because it is really only by taking part in a mediation that the importance of the private session can be appreciated. My company has several video films of mediations which took place in the United States in 1988 and were re-created immediately afterwards, with the actual participants playing themselves. These videos have helped put across to different audiences the importance of the caucus and the techniques used. Indeed, there was some levity when, addressing an important group of solicitors in September 1990, we showed one of these films about a central heating/construction litigation. At an important point when the mediator was testing the architect's case, he learned that one of the architect's key witnesses was unavailable for trial, having taken a job in Kuwait. We hadn't looked at this video since prior to the August 1990 invasion of that country.

The aim is to get the parties negotiating, but this shouldn't occur too early on. The reason for this is that the mediator must first get each side off its 'perch'. He must inject some reality before encouraging negotiation. Even before doing this, he must allow each side to talk in confidence about how they see the case and what they are really concerned about.

This first phase, which may last most of the first private session, involves the development of trust. The disputant is able to ventilate or get things off his chest and even though there is no great pay-off from persuading the mediator that their case is right, the parties frequently start by seeking to do this. A wise mediator will balance carefully the advantages of listening quietly, letting the relationship develop and the need to get the process going and move on to the other side.

The investigation stage

The next phase is to start asking tough questions. The aim is to extract each side's perception of its strengths and weaknesses and for the mediator then to use the exclusive knowledge he has of both cases to educate the parties. This must nevertheless be done in an impartial way, in order to maintain the trust that has been created. If possible, the questions must be asked with charm, or at least grace, since it is easy to overstep the mark and start to make one or other side think it is being heavily cross-examined. Furthermore, the mediator must normally avoid giving opinions, preferably not even letting anyone know what his views are. The reason is simple; if one side disagrees with your opinion, then he will think you are biased; if he agrees he will sooner or later impart this to the other side, who will think you are biased. The flow of information and rational argument, so vital in mediation, will dry up.

This need to be impartial makes things difficult, since most mediators are lawyers and lawyers are trained to analyse facts and law in order to form a conclusion. I was recently explaining the process to a distinguished barrister who said, 'I suppose I read the pleadings and expert's reports and then turn to one side and say, in relation to this or that issue, you can't seriously argue that a judge will find in your favour on . . . ?' He was nearly right but certainly during the early stages of the mediation it would be dangerous to use such strong language. The party concerned must actually agree with the point rather than feel pushed into a corner. He must agree in order that he will reassess his chances of success and therefore his BATNA (see page 3) and hence his bottom line or reserve position. There is more likelihood of movement if it is voluntary and accepted.

As always, there are exceptions to the rule. I think that as the mediation gathers momentum and the negotiations start buzzing, and they do, then there is a case for the mediator putting in his wooden spoon and stirring the mix with a few judicious comments. This is justified since the direction of the process is clear and, to change the metaphor, he is doing no more than clearing a few snags. Purist mediation theorists will no doubt disagree but the mediator is only human and wants a result almost as much as others. If he thinks it will be achieved more easily with a prod, so be it. This must not happen during the early phases, while trust is being built up and education about strengths and weaknesses is going on.

The other exception is when the process is breaking down. At a certain point (and with experience the mediator begins to feel whether there is a prospect of further movement in the negotiations or whether the parties are so far apart with their offers that the mediation is not going to achieve agreement without something unusual), there is nothing to lose by giving a firm and clear opinion, since deadlock is approaching. If the mediator is a recognised specialist or expert in the subject of the dispute or a distinguished lawyer, it could just be that his view will jolt one side into a re-assessment and get discussions going again. He is, after all, a third party with no interest in the outcome and this in itself gives him influence. Furthermore, he will normally give this opinion in confidence to one side, avoiding the risk of the other side crowing triumphantly. In one of the cases I mediated there were three parties, including an unrepresented civil engineer. Throughout the case he took the view that his *opinion* was *fact* and no judge could decide against him and go against fact. It was a case with the potential to go either way at trial – hence the other two parties wanted to settle. They began to make concessions but became frustrated when the engineer failed to recognise his risk.

I put him in with the first defendants who were, in an effort to reach a settlement, making larger concessions than they felt justified, simply because he wasn't moving with them and sharing the 'damages'. They gave him a roasting but he was obdurate. I then told him calmly that from what I had heard and with my experience of judges I thought the trial result would be against both defendants but that he would pay the greater proportion of the award *and* the costs. I had previously been making these points through the questioning technique but without much success. He was jolted by my expressing an opinion, coming right after the roasting from his fellow defendants, and shortly afterwards made a sufficient offer to encourage the plaintiff and the first defendants to settle their differences. My opinion was given after five and a half hours of mediation and I knew by then I couldn't get anywhere further using normal techniques with the engineer. After this he saw me as associated with the first defendants and, even more, the plaintiff. Had we not been in the area of settlement the tactic could have led to the end of the mediation without result.

Whilst he will not normally give opinions (nor answer questions) and should be neutral, the mediator must not allow himself to seem neutered. He is the chairman without a vote but he sets the agenda (allowing some flexibility) and the pace of the meeting. Having learned a bit about one party's strong points, he then goes to the other party and says (perhaps): 'The defendants tell me that despite the argument that you had no responsibility for supervision of the contract, your letter of the . . . refers to the fee covering site supervision. What effect will this letter have and what will be the worst outcome on this issue?' He might press further, suggesting a bad result on this issue might have a 'domino effect' on other issues. Note that there is no need to get a full essay-like answer, though most litigants would like to give one; the target is the plaintiff's own view of his case. To balance the 'grief', the mediator then learns about the plaintiff's strong points and carries the devil's advocacy back to the defendant.

At this stage, which involves education and reassessment, it is not usually sensible to probe too much into each side's settlement strategy and bottom line. At the end the mediator will push everyone as hard as he can towards their reserve positions; too early, though, and he may create difficulties for himself. This is because there hasn't yet been a full discussion of the case, as each side sees it, and of the risks of proceeding to trial. If a party declares his position too firmly early on, then he may get locked into an extreme position. Even though this declaration may be in caucus, and therefore confidential between the party and the mediator, there could still be a big loss of face, as between client and lawyer, militating against movement away from the extreme.

The negotiation stage

Depending on the complexity of the case and the number of issues, the mediator sooner or later reaches what I think of as the negotiating stage − or the mediation ends early. Using the confidentiality of the private sessions, the mediator asks the parties if they are ready to make an opening offer. Unsurprisingly, a degree of coyness about 'getting undressed first' creeps in here and it amuses me to see quite sophisticated litigants and their lawyers hop about trying to avoid the plunge, despite the fact they know that negotiation has got to start somewhere. One ploy is to get an assurance from one side that it will make concessions from the stated position but without quantifying by how much, then informing the other side of this, to encourage a definite offer. I should add that in some cases a prior difficulty is to get the defendant even to talk about quantum, since his view is that, not being liable, quantum is irrelevant.

A technique developed by Bryce Buehler, the USA&M office-holder for Arizona, Nevada and New Mexico, used in a mediation I saw recently in Las Vegas, is to invite each side in turn to offer a figure that is patently and openly not their best offer. The mediator informs the offeror that he will reveal to the offeree that it is not the best offer. He does exactly the same with the counter-proposal. In this way both sides feel comfortable. They have negotiating room. The mediator has, however, got them into the 'negotiating funnel'. He then steers them into the settlement zone:

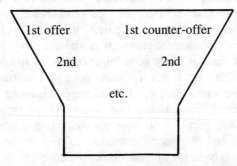

A danger of the funnel analogy is that a funnel is symmetrical, hence the idea can arise that settlement is always half way between the initial offers. This is not by any means always the result achieved, as a glance at case V in Appendix 5 will show.

Having overcome these hurdles and got the parties negotiating, the mediator has to develop and increase the momentum. The parties are receptive to settlement (unless they are cynically exploiting the system and are on a fishing exercise); the aim during the negotiating phase is to get them really to want to settle. This is not quite as bad as it sounds since the carrying back and forth of offers generates an impetus which can become exciting. Here lies a danger, in theory at least. What about the morning after? Will a party have been impelled towards a settlement which is not fair or not in its best interests?

This aims to be a practical book taking a look at the subject and giving a flavour. It is for the academics to consider in depth the issue of ethics. Advocates of mediation will riposte: 'People resolve their arguments all the time without recourse to any outside agencies; mediation involves no more than assisting them to their own solution. In neither instance can there be any guarantee that power will not prevail and that fairness will.' Nevertheless, the point is an important one. Some mediators are more forceful than others and a school of practitioners has developed in the United States known as 'muscle mediators'. Since any mediator seeks to stress weak points as well as strong ones, there is the risk that a party will overreact to pressure and concede too much. It will then be extremely difficult to extricate anyone from a binding agreement, reached after a voluntary meeting, especially if lawyers are present. There is no clear answer overall, but I do bear in mind the problems of pressure and influence in the mediations I do. Occasionally I take a step back to remind everyone that they are free to leave whenever they like, and there is no compulsion involved.

To return to the negotiations, there are a number of ways a mediator can close the gap (sometimes a variety of these methods will be used at the same time); these are as follows:

(1) Continue to stress the risks of not settling and analyse the cost implications, including irrecoverable costs. Sometimes the fact that up to one third of the costs are taxed off a winning side's costs is not known to the litigant and in cases where costs are a large part of the overall risk, this can make settlement wise, even when the prospects at trial are good. This is the sort of risk/cost/benefit analysis every good litigation lawyer should carry out with his client. The difference is that it is being done by a neutral.

(2) If the gap is small, the mediator will suggest splitting the difference.

(3) Explore creative solutions. This is not always possible in disputes which are between parties who have no continuing relationship, such as accident victims and insurance companies. In disputes between parties or companies who do business with each other regularly this is not so airy-fairy as might appear. In Appendix 5 the case history (No. VII) of two partners in dispute illustrates the point. The older retiring partner was pushing for as high a figure as he could get from the other partner, who was buying him out. The gap was too great and the first mediation session concluded without agreement, although the intervention of the mediator prevented vicious falling out and everyone agreed to meet again in six weeks' time. On the second occasion, the mediator saw the *need* of the older man to have sufficient money to retire with but the *need* of the younger man not to over-commit himself financially. The mediator suggested that the older man should continue to work for a further two years out of the company offices, rent free. The actual cost to the younger man was minimal but the solution increased the other's profits sufficiently to bridge the gap, a purchase price was agreed and the matter settled.

(4) Focus on the needs of the parties and away from rights/positions. It is inevitable that parties will be heavily influenced by their lawyers and will be looking at their case on the basis of what a court would be likely to award if they are successful on liability. What, though, do they want to use the money for? I recently did a mediation where a house owner was claiming damages from a surveyor for having failed to draw attention to dry rot in the roof timbers. The issues were not entirely straightforward but the surveyor was prepared to pay something to avoid a very expensive trial, which might have

lasted ten days. The discussion raged around values and the way a court awards damages in these cases. Then the house owner himself started to look at what he needed the money for − not in fact to re-do the timbers, since his wife had recently died, but to put a deposit down on a smaller property which was being offered at a discount for speedy exchange of contracts: quick settlement was worth more than a higher figure awarded considerably later.

(5) Use the 'last − best offer' technique. The idea is to ask each party for their bottom-line figure. They tell the mediator this in confidence and he stresses that he will not disclose the figure to the other side unless both sides' offers coincide or overlap, in which case settlement is achievable. Here it is vital for the mediator to extract the true bottom-line, since it would be regrettable if accord might be achieved, but isn't, owing to a lack of frankness by one side. If an overlap occurs, there could be a further squabble over that. The best course probably is for the mediator to return to each party and invite them to authorise him to split the difference.

If the parties are still apart, then an additional technique is to tell each side in turn that there is still a gap but it might be possible to close it. Each side is asked if they would like to know what the gap is up to a certain figure and if they would be prepared to split the difference up to that figure. The mediator cannot suggest the figure, since this would disclose the other side's bottom-line (add the difference to the bottom-line). If both come up with a figure for the gap which matches or is close, settlement can be achieved.

In a personal injury mediation I tried this technique with considerable success, but for all the wrong reasons. The plaintiff was a young lad whose resolve was stiffened by his canny father, who had previous experience of personal injury claims. The parties were still a long way apart and had reached an impasse. In desperation I thought of 'last-best'. Both lawyers saw the point and I got the defendant's figure. Just as the plaintiff's lawyer was going to give me his bottom-line, the father chipped in, '£42,000 and not a penny less . . . *give that* to the other side and see if it will make them move, then come back and I'll think about a further reduction.' The innocent statement of willingness to move allowed me, carefully, to suggest to the other side that the plaintiff might not be totally intransigent and this was enough to generate a better counter-offer from the defendant. We actually concluded a deal some time later having returned to straightforward negotiation.

(6) Generally encourage the parties, re-phrasing offensive messages and stressing positive aspects of the situation. In one case I felt reasonably confident it would settle but movement was slow. My confidence derived from the fact that no-one from the three sides was giving any sign of wanting to leave. I felt this was because everyone really wanted an agreement and there was therefore a lot more scope in the negotiations. I deliberately sought to convey my confidence that we would succeed. We did later reach agreement

and I attribute this in part to the right atmosphere being generated at a time when discussions had slowed down.

If settlement is reached, then an agreement is drawn up, often with everybody back together in joint session. If settlement is impossible, it is also standard mediation practice to bring all the participants together to thank them for trying and to recount the areas where some advance has been made. It is amazing how little true communication takes place during the litigation process and conversely how much each side learns about the other side's case, and what the real issues are, when they take part in a mediation. I am naturally disappointed when a mediation doesn't end with a result but I think it is worth while stressing the progress made. This is not simply being pious or self-congratulatory; many cases that don't settle on the day will do so at some time before trial and work done at mediation can be important for this. Issues are narrowed, issues and perceptions clarified. Occasionally the re-convening of the joint session will lead to renewed progress. Playing it by ear, the mediator might consider allowing the parties to re-state their case in five minutes, hoping that face-to-face dialogue might trigger fresh movement.

CHAPTER 3

The Legal and Ethical Status of Mediation and the Mediator

Since alternative dispute resolution and mediation are new to this country and do not, so far as I am aware (excluding arbitration), feature in case law or statute, a lot of the following discussion is going to fall short of being authoritative. Even in the United States the legal status of mediation is not fully developed, with some states having mediation laws and court-annexed schemes, while others ignore the subject. It is true however that a solicitor-mediator is covered by the Solicitors' Indemnity Fund Professional Indemnity Policy, as long as the fees go to his practice, and not to him personally. It is thought that even more so a solicitor-presenter is covered by the policy, as these are no more than assisted settlement negotiations.

Over here the Law Society's Professional Conduct Rules, at the time of writing, describe mediation as outside the normal practice of a solicitor and one has to fall back on general principles, in relation, for instance, to conflict of interest, for guidance on the subject.

I propose to look at the key elements (mediation is **voluntary, without prejudice, non-binding** and **confidential**) and then to look at possible difficulties and the documentation prepared by my company, IDR Europe Ltd, including a standard mediation clause, mediation procedures, an agreement to mediate and the mediator's letter confirming no bias and compliance with IDR procedures. All these documents are set out in the Appendices along with sample ADR clauses for contracts. I will then look at the mediator's legal status and touch on possible legal and ethical problems that could arise, such as negligence on the part of the mediator and fairness.

IDR Europe Ltd started life as a franchisee of United States Arbitration and Mediation, an American company with affiliated offices throughout the USA & Canada. Whilst the company has developed fresh ideas in its English setting, the documentation inherits a strong US flavour. It may be that over time this will change.

THE KEY ELEMENTS

Voluntary

Just as negotiations are voluntary, so is mediation. First, no-one has to consent to mediation clauses or, even less, agreements to mediate. Secondly, no mediation clause in a contract or even in an agreement to mediate reached after, say, intervention by an agency such as IDR can be enforced by specific performance. Either party can withdraw at any time, including a microsecond after the session has commenced.

This raises the question 'When does mediation commence?' In some ways it starts when one party refers the case to an agency or contacts the other party to suggest mediation. The process of persuading the other party to attend, when it is done by a third party such as IDR, CEDR or USA&M, usually involves mediatory techniques; and we have found negotiations actually taking place and cases settling before the date fixed for a meeting. Another view is that mediation commences when everyone signs an agreement to mediate. After that it is quite common for the mediator to speak by telephone to the parties, to introduce himself and ensure there are no unusual features in the case.

With that digression aside, I come back to the quality of voluntariness. I suppose it might be argued that with an imbalance in bargaining power, a contracting party may in reality be unable to avoid a mediation clause or a rent-review clause in a lease. But as I have said, the *process* is voluntary so no harm has been done, save that one or both sides may be precluded from issuing legal proceedings before a certain period has elapsed.

However, although there is no legal compulsion involved, there may be other forces at work which could put coercion on people to take part in mediation:

(1) Costs
(2) The pressure imposed by other parties agreeing to mediate
(3) The pressure imposed by 'sponsors'
(4) As the process develops, court recommendation or even, as in some states, court-ordered mediation.

I am sure there will be other forces or pressures but these four will suffice to illustrate possible problems. Problems because, as I indicated in the opening chapter, for a dispute to be appropriate for ADR and in particular mediation, there must be a basic willingness to take part and attempt a settlement. If there is coercion, even mild or hidden, the mediation may not get going or may become distorted.

Costs

Most litigators are familiar with the 'Calderbank offer', in other words a without-prejudice offer with the right reserved to make it open, if relevant, in the matter of costs, after a court decision. I can see a variation on this creeping into the mediation field. Thus a party may propose mediation in an open letter. This need not be seen as a concession, since a secondary but important aspect of the process is a thorough examination of the case by both sides. It is not only about final settlement negotiation. At a conference I recently attended on damages in business disputes, a London lawyer asked me if mediation was suitable for certain *parts* of large litigation cases. The answer is yes, if both parties have the right attitude. As the process becomes more widespread and better-known, there could be reference, made later in court, to a refusal to mediate. It could be argued, probably in conjunction with alleging other interlocutory misdemeanours (eg less than complete discovery), that the full rigour of the rules on costs should not necessarily be imposed on the losing party, if he genuinely tried to resolve the matter through mediation.

The scenario might at present seem far-fetched, but it is easier to reject a specific offer than a proposal to take part in a process which I think will increasingly prove its ability to bring about earlier settlements. It could be that judges will take note of the merits of mediation. The London Common Law and Commercial Bar Association proposal (page 10) includes a recommendation that although voluntary, the scheme put forward should sound in costs to the extent that a failure to take part could affect a later costs order.

Other parties

In multi-party cases one of the factors delaying settlement is the sheer difficulty of getting all the parties to communicate at the same level before the actual trial. Mediation gets them together before-hand and this factor alone makes it very useful in such cases. However, if one or two defendants agree to mediate, the third defendant who refuses is the odd man out, with all the pressures, including possible costs, that this entails. Additionally, the odd man out must fear ganging up against him by those parties who attend mediation.

Sponsors

Of more importance is the pressure that sponsors can apply. The term is used loosely to include insurers and other organisations who are paying the costs and/or have an interest in the outcome of the dispute. My experience to date is principally with insurers; however, the question of legal aid is likely to enter gradually into the whole debate about ADR, and in this context one can foresee parties being the subject of a condition of their legal aid certificate that further steps in the litigation require an offer to mediate first.

At the moment London & Edinburgh Insurance and the Solicitors' Indemnity Fund are referring cases to mediation. A number of other insurers are following their lead. Sometimes the indemnified has a separate interest from the insurer, particularly where there is a large policy excess. It is normal for the insurer to have the last word on how to deal with a dispute and this might lead to slightly disgruntled participants in the mediation. This is not necessarily undesirable, since once there the indemnified may well derive benefit from the process.

Courts

It may be that courts will eventually have the power to order mediation. The trouble will be the 'horse to water' syndrome. You cannot force a party to negotiate, and imposed and involuntary mediation may start off on the wrong footing. Another disadvantage is that if the process becomes institutionalised and relatively badly paid, then mediators of mixed quality will turn up and mediation will get a bad name.

To conclude this section, if mediation is not quite as voluntary as it might seem, that is not wholly undesirable. The process is often useful, and initially unwilling participants can be surprised at what happens. There is risk, however, that cost pressures and even more, court-ordered mediation could lead to 'lip-service' participation and create the wrong attitude, with the result that the mediator's task is made harder and perhaps impossible. There may, though, be scope for the court to select suitable cases to recommend the mediation and pilot schemes are to be encouraged.

Non-binding

Unless med-arb (see page 8) or some similar scheme is involved, mediation is clearly non-binding. If the parties reach agreement, they can, subject to comments I make below, bind themselves either contractually or with a consent order such as a Tomlin Order. (This is an order named after Judge Tomlin. The normal contents are a provision for the action to be discontinued but only on the basis that the terms of the schedule are fully complied with.) This is no different from the traditional 'face to face' settlement negotiation. A Tomlin Order has the merit of allowing the parties to build into an agreement various different factors, including enforcement in the event of a non-compliance. It has been suggested that even if proceedings have not been issued, it could be part of an agreement that a writ will be issued, in order to be able to achieve a Tomlin Order.

It is the non-binding element in the process that encourages the parties to open up with the mediator, since they know that information disclosed will not directly affect the result. (This argument also applies to confidentiality). It is a strength of mediation, but in the wrong cases can be a weakness. This highlights, again, the point about attitude; the inability of the mediator to give a decision means that he will only succeed (as far as settlement is concerned) with those parties who want to settle, those parties who have a basic propensity to settle but for various reasons are as yet unable to.

Without prejudice and confidential

Without prejudice is a term which has given rise to numerous arguments over the years and doubtless it will at some stage engender litigation relating to mediation. So far so good, however.

The way it and confidentiality operate in practice is that every stage is deemed to be without prejudice and the agreement to mediate includes specific provision that the mediator shall not be called to give evidence or produce documents or other information or materials either in court or at an arbitration or other adjudicative tribunal. The mediation session is described as a settlement negotiation, and as such without prejudice. All documents and other materials disclosed must either be returned to the originating party or destroyed, at that party's option. Everything learned must be treated confidentially and this applies equally to the mediator, as to the parties.

Some guidance as to the interpretation likely to be applied by the courts can be gleaned from family law and the area of conciliation and reconciliation negotiation. The case of *McTaggart v McTaggart* [1948] 2 All ER 754, CA is authority for the proposition that communications made in the course of negotiations for reconciliation are privileged and cannot generally be admitted in evidence without the parties' consent. The privilege belongs to the parties and not the conciliator. A later case, *Henley v Henley* [1955] 1 All ER 590, decided that the privilege applies, whether the initiative for reconciliation comes from one of the parties or the conciliator himself. It is not strictly necessary for the proceedings and documents produced to be marked 'without prejudice' but this does depend on what the courts have called a tacit understanding. I came across the problem at a mediation where tempers were already frayed. One of the solicitors had hold of the other side's opening summary and was contending that as it was not marked without prejudice he was entitled to use it in evidence. The mediation had been clearly stated to be without prejudice and the agreement to mediate extended this to all documents; however, for the avoidance of doubt I asked for all copies of the document to be marked accordingly. I recommend that, as in that case, wherever there is an intention to leave copies of documents with other parties, then they should be expressly marked without prejudice, if it is intended that they should be so treated.

Thus, the mediator cannot, strictly, be called to give evidence if there is a dispute as to the meaning of an 'agreement' reached. Still less can he be called to support one side if there is no agreement reached. Nor can the parties themselves refer to what happened in the process. There is some uncertainty as to the situation where agreement is reached but the parties later fall out over technical issues. Without prejudice 'falls away' on the parties reaching agreement. However, the process is also confidential and it might be argued that it is only the agreement itself that is 'open' — all that went before should remain 'closed'. These provisions are important, to get the parties to go to the mediation and to generate the trust necessary to get communication and negotiation going. They are jealously guarded by those involved in mediation. There are, however, certain exceptions to the confidentiality rule: the most obvious is that relating to criminal conduct by the parties or an agreement which is or may become illegal. Other exceptions could arise where an agreement is reached on the basis of false information or as a result of negotiations conducted in bad faith. Quite how these exceptions sit with the wording of the agreement to mediate and the mediation procedures has yet to be seen but naturally the agreement cannot override duties owed by the mediator under the criminal law.

Both as a matter of good mediation practice and to protect himself from charges of condoning illegality, the mediator should, in circumstances of possible illegality, seek to rectify the problem. If the parties wish to maintain their agreement, then he should withdraw and terminate the mediation. He will then have to wrestle with his conscience as to whether he notifies the authorities; particularly if he is a lawyer he may find the appropriate guidance in the ethical code of the Bar and solicitor's professional rules. Ideally, the mediator should sense that a problem is going to arise, well before it materialises. He can then withdraw before actual agreement is reached. To assist him, IDR has provided a clause to the effect that the mediator may withdraw without giving any reason.

Under the IDR system the mediator does not sign the agreement to mediate but confirms that he is bound by the agreement and the current IDR mediation procedures. He declares his impartiality and that the confidentiality conditions apply to him.

POSSIBLE DIFFICULTIES

The mediation procedures (Appendix 1) expressly state that the mediator does not act as a lawyer and has no duty to 'analyse or protect any legal right'. What then is his status in law? He is not a judge or arbitrator and there is no decision to be appealed against nor can there be a failure to follow correct procedures to initiate the same process.

He is in fact an 'intermeddler'. This is not a precise legal category but the word certainly has unfortunate connotations. Two's company, three's a crowd . . . and so on. On a personal level he suffers from this: if the case settles, then everyone feels it was a natural result with no particular credit due to the mediator, it would have happened anyway; if the case doesn't settle, the mediator didn't do his job well enough. On a legal level he cannot escape a duty to the parties to take 'reasonable care' and to comply with contractual requirements such as confidentiality and impartiality.

False information

There seem to be a number of areas where he could go wrong and to reflect this IDR has arranged E & O cover for each of its panel mediators, to take effect if they are not already covered by their own professional indemnity policy. The following problems may arise:

(1) The mediator is given information that he is asked to convey to the other side but which he fails to convey.

(2) He is given information which he passes on inaccurately, by mistake.

(3) He passes on information which he is told in confidence and has been specifically asked to keep from the other side.

(4) Perhaps less likely, he conveys information neither party has given to him and which is without foundation in fact.

(5) The mediator deliberately lies in order to manipulate one or both parties to reach agreement.

It seems quite fair and just that a mediator should be judged by, and should measure up to, the standards that apply to other professionals. He may not be a lawyer but he is chairing an important meeting for the parties and a mistake or deliberate misfeasance on his part could have serious repercussions. In the United States there is an organisation called SPIDR – the Society for Professionals in Dispute Resolution. It aims to set standards and develop a professional attitude and approach. There is now a branch of this Society in England. If a mediator, or other ADR practitioner, aspires to the status of professional, there is a corresponding duty of care and standard of practice and behaviour.

If the parties reach an agreement and one or both have relied upon information which is inaccurate and the inaccuracy can be attributed to the mediator, there seems no reason why he should not be liable for such loss as may be suffered. The law of mistake may apply and indeed rectification may be available or a setting aside of the whole agreement.

Another scenario is that a party deliberately feeds false information to the mediator which is acted on by the other side and an unfair agreement reached. What if the mediator ought to have determined that this information was false?

This is not an easy point and there are no cases anywhere in the world, yet, to help. On the one hand there is the specific disclaimer in the IDR mediation procedures (Appendix 1) that the mediator is not acting as a lawyer nor has he a duty to analyse the issues nor to protect either party independently. Also, the parties are, normally, separately legally represented. On the other hand the law in this country has begun to scrutinise exclusion clauses carefully. The Unfair Contract Terms Act 1977 and the Supply of Goods and Services Act 1982 are examples of legislation impinging on the subject. Furthermore, a mediator is sometimes selected for his expert knowledge in the subject-matter of the dispute. This is likely to raise the standard of care in those situations where a duty can be established.

Fairness

In the above instance of a mediator failing to spot deliberate falsehood there is an ethical issue in addition to a legal one. What is the mediator's duty, expressed in ethical terms, to the concept of fairness? When it is looked at as a method of dispute resolution compared with litigation, which actually gets resolved by the court, there are grounds for thinking that mediation has weaknesses. Litigation has developed over many years with precise checks and balances, introduced by legislation or rule-making and developed by case law. Put at its highest, the judiciary is a vital element in the constitutional freedom of the individual. Mediation has no such built-in and well-developed checks and balances. It is perhaps not sufficient simply to argue that mediation is assisted negotiation and the parties reach their own conclusion. This is a new process and is being promoted as an alternative to litigation. Parties resorting to mediation may, therefore, place greater reliance on the process and the mediator, to obtain a fair result without intimidation and economic pressure, than on the old face-to-face bargaining process.

The answer to this criticism is on serveral different levels:

(1) Most litigation settles without having relied on the checks and balances to the full, anyway.

(2) Some mediation results are subject to legal review. This is often necessary in matrimonial cases and any litigation involving children. It is also potentially available under the rules of natural justice and the doctrines of mistake and rectification.

(3) The principal agent of fairness is a skilled and reasonable mediator.

To assist in producing skilled and reasonable mediators, and in addition to mediation procedures, IDR has developed a code of conduct for professional mediators. This is derived from codes written in the United States, where this issue of fairness is debated at length. CEDR also has a code of conduct. There is also a need to ensure that mediation training is thorough and that performance is reviewed from time to time.

The mediator's purpose is to assist the parties in assessing their strengths and weaknesses in order to enable them to make realistic negotiation decisions based upon, so far as possible, an objective evaluation of their case and the likely outcome of alternatives to settlement, usually litigation. A dominant feature of this approach is reasonableness. Therefore, the mediator is more likely than not to promote fairness, though it must be said that he cannot be a guarantee of it. He is not there to add his weight to the 'weaker side', to seek to balance the arguments. He is there to get the argument to a realistic level.

What should a mediator do if he perceives that an imbalance between the negotiating strengths of the parties means that litigation is more likely to lead to a *fair* settlement than continuing the mediation, sensing at the same time that a mediated agreement is round the corner? Negotiating strength or power derives from a variety of sources, including knowledge and experience, and it is not merely economic. The Center for Dispute Resolution, Denver, Colorado Code of Professional Conduct for Mediators refers, *inter alia*, to 'Appropriatness of Mediation'. It goes on to say:

'Mediators should be aware of all procedures for dispute resolution and under what conditions each is most effective. Mediators are obliged to educate participants as to their procedural options and help them make wise decisions as to the most appropriate procedures. The procedures should clearly match the type of outcome which is desired by the parties'.

If that is right, then the mediator has a difficult choice in the hypothetical situation set out above. In extreme cases he really must ask questions directed at guiding the parties to litigation and may even terminate the mediation. The situation, fortunately, may not be that stark and one mediation I did threw up similar considerations.

The plaintiff and its solicitors were not specialists in the particular type of litigation involved and were, it became apparent, unaware that the proper conduct of the plaintiff's case required that a specialist report should be obtained dealing with one aspect of the dispute. I was given, in confidence, the range of figures within which Counsel had advised the plaintiff should settle. The defendants and their legal advisers were aware of the defect in the other side's case and for a time were conducting the negotiations on the basis that, as this particular aspect of the dispute was not raised, their offers were low. However, I was instructed by them not to disclose the weakness in the other side's case preparation. This could have become very awkward and mediator ethics became a live issue for me. As it happened, the defendants realised, partly through prompting, that if they held out for too low a figure, then there could be no settlement and on resumption of litigation the barrister would be likely to advise on evidence and hence the report would be obtained. The defendants increased their offer significantly and happily for me, the case settled within the plaintiff's range. The plaintiff and their solicitors never discussed my dilemma and I believe everyone was satisfied. I consider that had settlement been imminent below the plaintiff's original acceptable range, then my first course of action should have been to discuss the problem in confidence with the defendants and indicate my difficulties in clear terms. If that had failed, I might have had to terminate the mediation. That would have been very unsatisfactory and against my instincts − I wanted a result and there would have been no guarantee of correction to the defect. The problem is posed here, but not solved.

If any one conclusion can be drawn from the consideration of legal and ethical issues in this chapter, it is that mediators must develop codes of conduct and standards of professionalism. They must be selected and trained not only for legal and technical skill, and for personality, but also for a willingness to appreciate and address difficult issues and maintain high standards in this area. A failure here will leave mediation marginal and without the respect of the legal world it greatly needs.

CHAPTER 4

Mediation from the Lawyer's Point of View

'A lawyer has no business with the justice or injustice of the cause which he undertakes, unless the client asks his opinion, and then he is bound to give it honestly.' – Dr Johnson

Lawyers, and particularly barristers, are trained to be disinterested in the traditional sense of the word. That is, they are to some extent impartial and neutral. They owe a duty to the legal system as well as to the client. This ought to give them a good background to take part in mediation both as representatives of parties in conflict, and as mediators. I shall deal with the particular role of the lawyer as a mediator in a later chapter, but it is my view that the future of ADR and commercial mediation (as opposed to family mediation) in this country is closely tied up with the attitude of solicitors and barristers towards it, and the involvement of both as representatives and mediators.

This is because the most dramatic impact of ADR is going to be in the area of disputes that have already gone legal. The experience of my company, IDR Europe Ltd, over the last eighteen months has shown that the vast majority of the cases referred for mediation have already commenced life in the courts. The Lord Chancellor has regularly endorsed ADR as a means of saving time and money and both the Law Society and the Bar Council are looking actively at ADR and mediation schemes. A national network of fifteen or so well respected firms of solicitors, ADR Net Ltd, has been set up to train lawyer mediators and provide ADR and mediation promotion. The Centre for Dispute Resolution (CEDR) has been set up by leading firms of lawyers with pledges from members, including national companies and institutions, to take part in ADR procedures before resorting to litigation amongst themselves. The British Academy of Experts has also initiated an ADR project which leans closely into the legal profession.

It should not be thought, however, that lawyers will have it all their own way. Mediation purists here and in the United States are of the view that lawyers are not necessary to the process and can be detrimental to it. The argument is that the ADR movement grew up largely as a response to the defects in the litigation dispute-resolution system and many of these defects are attributable to the attitudes and behaviour of lawyers. Lawyers are seen as running cases longer than necessary to generate costs and, in the United States, to share a larger slice of damages. They are naturally adversarial.

To some extent these criticisms have application in this country, although the lack of a contingency fee system and the rule that costs follow the event are both encouragements to settlement not present in America. Certainly, however, there is a common enough view among corporate and individual disputants that, being expensive and risk-laden, litigation and resort to lawyers should be avoided if at all possible.

These ADR purists go on to argue that the aim of ADR is to blunt the adversarial edge and to be quicker and less expensive than arbitration and litigation. Lawyers by their training and experience are adversarial. Lawyers focus on *rights* (positions) rather than interests; they have to build up enough 'points' to score a victory. Mediators, however, concentrate on *interests* and *needs* in order to solve problems and in doing so dig deeper into the dispute than lawyers are able and also attempt to defuse unnecessary conflict.

An illustration of this argument might be the case of the factory owner whose building is defective and who makes a claim against the main contractor and a variety of sub-contractors. By virtue of it being a multi-party action it is inevitably going to take years rather than months to resolve. Armed with opinions from experts and Counsel and an aggressive solicitor, the factory owner considers the law is with him and his position is 'Pay up or I'll take you to court.' His thought processes and those of his lawyers become fixed in that direction. He might settle for less than his claim as a premium against litigation but the logistics of getting a deal with so many parties are difficult. The case marches inexorably to trial.

The mediator, on the other hand, whilst examining the legal and factual position and the plaintiff's likely achievement if the case goes to trial, also concentrates on interests and needs. He discovers that one of the defendants is a man of straw which adds to the risks both on damages and costs. He asks what the damages are needed for and discovers that the intention is not to rebuild the factory, since it has been patched up pending planned demolition and a large part of the extensive forecourt car park is to be sold for development. The money will be used for the acquisition of shares in another company which are currently under-priced. When the dispute is looked at in this light, the plaintiff may well consider making much larger concessions, as against his perceived legal right, in order to get a quick settlement without the need for difficult enforcement and the need to disguise his intention to demolish.

In reality there is no reason why a lawyer cannot be just as imaginative as the hypothetical mediator in the foregoing illustration. Many lawyers practise in a conciliatory way as far as the system allows. Furthermore, the lawyers present at the above hypothetical mediation may well have considered a lot of these points and discussed them with their respective clients. However, some education and training in the subject of ADR and specifically mediation is essential. Lawyers need to be made more aware of the ADR approach and the particular skills needed to practice either as a representative or a mediator.

There are cases which are more suitable for non-lawyers; the partnership dispute referred to in Appendix 5 on page 111 was mediated by Andrew Fraley, Training Director of IDR Europe Ltd, who is not a lawyer, though an excellent and imaginative mediator. No lawyers were present for either partner even though the money in issue stood at several hundred thousand pounds. One of the problems was a quarrel over a complicated share agreement which in the event was disregarded and in many ways the absence of a lawyer gave the negotations more flexibility than there might otherwise have been. This was a case that had not reached litigation, but which might have, in the absence of agreement.

There are good arguments for developing ADR and mediation schemes within different sectors of the economy and public life, to be operated, largely, by people from within these sectors. In other words non-lawyers. The British Medical Association is developing just such a scheme to give doctors in practice together the option of referring disputes to mediation. Approximately 10 per cent of doctors practising together move on each year, with the result that finance and restrictive covenants have to be negotiated. The BMA scheme aims to train doctor mediators who, knowing their profession and the problems that occur, are best able to bring about positive solutions that are acceptable to all and preserve relationships. IDR Europe Ltd is working with the Retail Credit Group to bring about a mediation scheme for disputes between consumers/customers and the suppliers of credit in the retail field. Lawyers are unlikely to be involved here.

However, the mediations I have done or been associated with in this country have mostly been in respect of cases with writs already issued, with lawyers instructed on both sides. I am convinced that the involvement of lawyers in those mediations was vital and that settlement in those cases where this has been achieved (82 per cent) would have been far less likely without legal representation. Set out below are some of the issues that will face the lawyer taking part in mediation.

WHY MEDIATION?

This will be an important question asked by the lawyers considering alternatives to litigation and being aware of mediation. It will also be a question asked by the lawyer invited to take part in a mediation, the other side having referred the case.

The specific advantages of the process are dealt with in other parts of this book. Perhaps the simplest answer to the question is that mediation usually works more quickly than either litigation or face-to-face negotiation . . . in those cases where settlement at the end of the day is likely and where there is a basic willingness on both sides to consider a settlement.

This speed factor in turn means that, even with the costs of mediation, a better result can be achieved by both parties than by for example, a court-door settlement, and a considerable amount of legal and managerial expense can be saved. Since 90 per cent of cases issued in the High Court settle before trial or at the court door, in the vast majority of cases the time comparison is between a mediation result and settlement after some litigation and not between mediation and the result of a trial or trials.

Clearly, there will be cases that settle face-to-face before issue of process and those that settle face-to-face in no more time than it would take to mediate – mediation is not a panacea. However, there is a considerable number of cases that rumble on and on, going through each interlocutory stage with more or less speed and vigour. These are the cases which could well benefit from mediation, not because the plaintiff or defendant is likely to get a higher or lower settlement figure, but because mediation brings negotiations to a head more quickly and effectively.

WHAT CASES ARE SUITABLE?

At a recent conference of solicitors at which ADR was being discussed, a thoughtful member of the audience said, 'It's simply the attitude of the parties – if they want to settle, any case is appropriate'.

That generalisation needs further consideration since mediation is not necessarily the appropriate dispute resolution method in all cases where there is the right attitude (face-to-face negotiation may be cheaper), and there is also the secondary question of *when* to use it in those cases where it is appropriate.

I propose to look at suitability under the sub-headings set out below. Before I turn to them, I would make two observations. First, there is no academic study anywhere in the world that has taken sets of otherwise identical cases and put one set through litigation, another through arbitration, and so on, in order to establish, empirically, the most effective method of resolving disputes of different types. Because ADR is new in this country, any assertions made below are bound to be even more tentative than views based on American experiences, which, in part, support the following analysis. Secondly, in many cases the lawyer will also be looking at methods other than mediation. I would urge an early analysis of dispute resolution strategy in *any* dispute, to maximise the client's prospects of getting a satisfactory result.

The different matters to consider when deciding if a case is suitable for mediation include some or all of the following:
(1) Relationships between the parties
(2) Power balance between the parties
(3) Size of the dispute
(4) Subject matter of dispute

(5) How the case is being handled by clients and lawyers
(6) The stage reached.

(1) Relationship

Mediation is all the more useful in those cases (see Appendix 5) where a continuing relationship needs to be maintained. This could be so between business partners, even on dissolution, because distribution of business goodwill and winding up require co-operation. It could be so between companies that regularly do business with each other. It may be that cases falling into this category will not come so frequently to the litigation department, since very often the client has given up on the relationship with his opponent when he instructs a solicitor to sue. On the other hand, many non-contentious departments come across incipient disputes which might well be suitable for mediation before they are passed across to the litigators. Accountants appear to be better at this informal approach to disputes than solicitors, looking to preserve relationships between their clients, for obvious reasons. They may find mediation a useful tool in this context. Commercial departments in legal firms should look at problems with ADR in view.

Just because the parties have no continuing relationship, as in a personal injury claim between plaintiff and insurer, by no means rules out mediation or other non-adjuduicatory methods; other factors apply in such cases. However, relationship cases are naturally suitable for mediation, at a very early point, to minimise the damage litigation can cause.

(2) Power balance

Where there is a wide disparity between the parties, in terms of power, then mediation may not be suitable. The sole plaintiff, even if legally aided, is unlikely to want to negotiate individually with a large government department, or water authority, even in the 'sympathetic' environment of a mediation session. Groups of such plaintiffs still face severe problems with such opponents and are likely to need the protection afforded by a court decision in a class action. It could be, however, that once a court decision has been obtained, mediation is appropriate to sort out the level of damages in other and later cases. In this situation the claimant is part of the decision-making process and the power balance is redressed by the earlier decision. I understand that in one medical negligence situation, where there was a class of claimants/ plaintiffs, it was decided by the defendant to instruct leading counsel to negotiate each claim with leading counsel 'offered' to claimants for free, as a way of avoiding the expense and risk of litigation. There was not a large take-up of the offer and one of the reasons given was that the claimants felt they were too far removed from the decision-making process in resolving their claim. Mediation avoids this problem.

(3) Size of dispute

In theory, there is no reason why the largest and the smallest cases should not be mediated. In practice, certain matters intrude which have to be taken into account. In *large cases*, say over a million pounds, the ratio of claim to costs could well make litigation relatively more attractive. Secondly, there are not yet enough suitably experienced mediators in this country who will feel comfortable with claims of this size, and in whom the parties will put the necessary trust and respect. Thirdly, a number of large cases fall into recognisable categories, such as construction disputes, with established alternatives to litigation. Construction cases are often dealt with by arbitration and it may be some time before those involved in the decision-making are prepared to consider mediation. I recall one case which was referred to IDR Europe by the main contractor in a construction dispute, only to be rejected by the employer, whose professional advisers insisted that it should be arbitrated. One reason for this approach, as well as entrenched views and vested interests, is that delay can of course be a vital factor in choice of dispute resolution. The company with large commercial buildings recently constructed, but no tenants, is quite happy to litigate or arbitrate for several years, to avoid the situation of paying the claim without the cash flow to meet the payment.

Small cases are equally suitable in theory, particularly small cases with complex facts and law. However, cases worth less than one or two thousand pounds may not be economically dealt with by mediation, unless specific low-cost schemes are available. IDR has set up such a scheme in conjunction with the Bristol Chamber of Commerce. Mediations do not always succeed and there is the additional cost of the mediation, legal fees for the time spent at the mediation and the client's other costs of preparing and attending the session. A number of schemes, such as the one with the Retail Credit Group, are being set up with mediators whose charges are less than the usual fees. The idea is to get parties together with a mediator who knows the subject-matter and to resolve the dispute within an hour or so. It is interesting, in this context, to note that telephone mediation is now being used by the Solicitors' Complaints Bureau, with mediators trained by IDR Europe Ltd. Another initiative is the mediation of debt collection by the Bristol Chamber of Commerce; the aim here is to establish early on the reason for non-payment, in order that the creditor can decide whether to sue in the courts and possibly lose his business relationship, or whether the non-payment is due to inability to pay, in which case why throw good money after bad? This nicely illustrates a key feature of mediation: improving communication between the parties. It has nothing to do with trying to negotiate the amount of the debt.

For the next few years it is likely that mediated cases will fall within the range between about £5,000, and perhaps £500,000. Mini-trials are generally more suitable for larger corporate disputes involving, as they do, a bit more formality, the opportunity to test evidence and the presence of senior executives to make key decisions.

There will always be exceptions at either end of the spectrum. One particular category of case deserves some mention. This is the claim of low value which is very expensive to prosecute. A variant is the low-value claim which might bring about a huge counter-claim; an instance of this being the claim for professional fees by, say, an architect or solicitor against a disgruntled client. It is by no means uncommon for the architect to sow the wind of a fees claim and reap the whirlwind of a counter-claim for breach of contract and negligence. Caught at the right moment early on and the other side being willing, these cases are very suitable for mediation. Either they will settle, in which case the disproportionate costs are avoided, or the mediation session clarifies the issues in order that one or other party can make a better informed decision as to whether to risk continuing litigation and how to conduct it.

(4) Subject-matter of dispute

American academics talk about integrative and distributive bargaining. Simply put, the former involves a number of different issues where it is possible to get both parties to a win/win situation, and the latter involves 'one more for me is one less for you' or zero sum. Naturally, the win/win type of case is highest on the list of suitability for mediation. Sometimes one or more issues are beyond the jurisdiction of a judge or arbitrator and a decision on one aspect only can be very harmful to future relations and not a little costly. Nevertheless, a lot of litigation cases fall into the distributive category inasmuch as they boil down to amounts of money being claimed and the zero sum formula applies. There is no reason why these cases are not also suitable as long as the related factors point in the same direction.

From the huge array of disputes I propose to select and look at some types to see whether they are suitable. This exercise is far short of comprehensive and in some ways its purpose is to set off a train of thought in the mind of the reader, not to produce a taxonomy of disputes.

Boundary disputes are notorious for being expensive and corrosive of neighbourly relations. They are loathed by judges and lawyers alike. They often illustrate the aphorism that it is a mistake to litigate over matters of principle i.e. to stand by rights and positions at the price of losing out on real needs and interests. They are generally suitable for mediation, though even as a confirmed advocate of the process I don't believe they will always be easy to resolve. There is a premium on preserving relationships if only to avoid the preliminary enquiry 'What is the dispute about?' The cost often greatly outweighs the value of the land in question to the point that in one legal aid case the statutory charge in respect of costs crippled the successful defendant who preserved an inch of land but didn't get all his costs.

In the right type of boundary dispute there should be sufficient options for a persuasive and imaginative mediator to take the parties away from the distributive mould. Thus, a concession as to the boundary line could be matched by an improvement in a right of way and an agreement as to cutting hedges. Too often the lawyers, either by instinct or to satisfy the client that they are taking up the cudgels vigorously enough, will become aggressively blinkered to the needs of the parties as opposed their rights.

Personal injury cases can also be suitable. This applies both to those cases where liability is also in issue, and to those where quantum is the only area of disagreement. A number of ADR companies provide useful guidelines as to how to identify 'mediable' cases – these include such phrases as 'It has been over 3 months since the parties discussed settlement' or 'Your phone calls or letters go unanswered by the other side' or 'You are having client-control problems'. How often do these and other common problems arise in personal injury litigation?

Timing is important in these cases. The injury may not have settled down sufficiently for a final medical report or the claim may not have been accurately quantified. The different stages of litigation require time and effort. The injury takes time to heal. The plaintiff's lawyer delays and periodically has to refresh his memory as to arguments and facts. Money is paid into court and if not accepted, is soon forgotten about. These cases can easily become skeletons in the cupboard.

In fact many personal injury claims are relatively straightforward and very mediable. Perhaps the greatest single advantage of the process is the fact that for the first time all the relevant people get together with the necessary authority/capacity to reach an agreement. Normally this only happens at trial, since interlocutory applications do not bring the claimant into contact with the insurer/defendant. Once together, it is not too difficult for the parties to start negotiating. There may be a number of medical and financial issues; there may be considerable divergence of views about liability and contributory negligence; but on the assumption that both parties would like a settlement if it is within their acceptable range, then it is remarkable how concessions come about.

I think this is because the impartial and sympathetic approach of the mediator encourages candour. The confrontational situation, which normally exists in litigation, does not encourage openness. For negotiations to work (a) they need to commence, (b) they need to develop and (c) they need to reach a conclusion. Parties communicating by way of desultory correspondence do not even like to put a figure on how they value their case, let alone make an opening offer. The mediator can be a bit like a father confessor; once the reluctance to communicate has been overcome, the parties actually enjoy talking about their case. It is not then such a large step for the mediator to encourage openness about value and, later, the first tentative moves towards an offer. If there is reciprocation from the other side, there is usually a good chance of settlement. Closing the deal is a bit more awkward; certain techniques are referred to in Chapter 6; above all, the mediator's personality is important and an ability to close does not simply require analytical and good communication skills. The mediator has to make the parties feel comfortable with a settlement.

Professional indemnity litigation is also, potentially, an area from which suitable cases can be selected. The issues are often by no means clear-cut and therefore advising clients what the likely result will be is not easy. There is sometimes a premium on privacy. Often the indemnified's lawyer is balancing the interests and requirements of the insurer and the client. For all these reasons, a mediation can be very useful. I was involved in one case where a dissatisfied businessman issued a writ against both solicitor and surveyor in relation to a property transaction. Prior to the mediation one of the defendants had taken the view that delay was a sensible tactic, believing the plaintiff might lose heart with the strain of litigation. The other defendant felt there was a risk and wanted to discuss settlement and avoid the expenses of trial. An added complication was that with a substantial excess, the second defendant had a genuine interest in the result of the litigation and there was, to a degree, a separate issue between insured and indemnified – the insurer was considering settlement, the professional was standing on his dignity, being reluctant to concede any fault. The mediation was difficult and did not achieve settlement on the day. I learned some months later that at least one of the parties had nevertheless felt the process had been very useful both in terms of encouraging a common view of the case by both defendants, and in terms of clarifying the issues in dispute and the real way the case was being argued (as opposed to the way it was being pleaded). It subsequently settled well before trial.

This case also illustrates that mediation can be suitable for cases characterised not by the subject-matter so much as the number of parties and different interests involved. With three parties and potentially conflicting interests between insurers and defendants, the mediation forum provided a practical way of speeding up and improving communication. This argument is even stronger with multi-party actions. Even when one of the parties in such cases is prepared to risk being thought weak and is prepared to do the hard work of organising a meeting, it is far more likely that a neutral organisation or party can successfully arrange such a meeting. At the moment it is only the court, with pre-trial reviews, appointments before the Official Referee and so forth, that acts as a 'neutral' encouraging meetings between all the parties. More often than not these appointments are wasted, rarely taking settlement, rather than the litigation, forward.

(5)   How the case is being handled

This applies to both sides, or all sides in multi-party cases. Discussing personal injury cases above (page 43), I mentioned common problems of delay and failure to respond to letters and telephone calls. This can indicate that the solicitor on the other side has problems; he might be over-worked; he could be having difficulty managing his client; or he might be slightly out of his depth.

In all the above examples the delay is not primarily due to the nature of the case, or to the litigation process, but to the attitude and capacity of the personalities, lawyers and clients. This problem is not confined to personal injury cases. In the 'driest' of commercial cases, with insurers and corporate clients, there can still be underlying non-legal problems holding up a realistic appraisal and effort to settle. This can be for such reasons as personal animosity between the solicitors conducting the files or difficulties between the claims manager for the insurer and its solicitors. If a case is otherwise mediable, in other words if it is a case which 'should settle', at some stage lawyers for the plaintiff and the defence ought to consider mediation when these delays occur.

The mediation agency asked to intervene and set up the mediation is often more successful in getting communication going and the presence of a deadline (the mediation session), albeit not imposed, encourages the swifter preparation of reports and schedules which are necessary for either settlement or trial. It is an interesting fact that IDR Europe Ltd has been instrumental in settling a number of cases simply by virtue of having made a few telephone calls.

If the problems are centred around 'client control', then a mediation session will probably be necessary. The careful analysis of the facts and arguments, with frequent measuring against reality, encourages difficult clients to reduce their expectations and demands. It is one thing to talk to the client in your office and recite the strong points of the case; it is quite another thing for the client to hear the strong points of the other side's case put across by the neutral and sensible mediator. It is a common feature of taking litigation instructions and advising a client that the lawyer has to strike a balance between a careful analysis according to legal principles and a vigorous commitment to contesting the case as hard as possible. Inevitably, there is a tendency to veer more toward vigour than academic analysis, since the lawyer has to satisfy his client that he is an adequate champion and not a mouse-like technician. Sometimes clients extend their requirements to specific matters: 'Make their life difficult, don't agree to an inspection, force then to make application to the court . . .' Mediation can be a way forward in this type of situation, either for the lawyer whose client is being difficult or for the lawyer who sees that the other side's client has a problem. The client might well reject common sense communicated by the other side, simply because of where it comes from. It is much more difficult, though not impossible, to reject it from a respected neutral. This can also apply to an over-zealous lawyer.

(6)   The stage reached

If a case is suitable in general terms, or displays some of the signs referred to above, there is still the question of *when* to attempt mediation. The following stages may be appropriate for an initiative.

First, if a writ is about to be issued, then a lawyer should consider whether mediation is possible. The greatest savings that can be obtained from mediation come from avoiding litigation altogether. Secondly, discovery is about to take place. In itself the discovery process is sometimes used by lawyers as an opportunity to float settlement ideas. It is also a point at which to consider ADR. The chances are that the key issues of the case are being thought about in order to decide which documents are discoverable and how the other side's documents help or hinder the argument. Contact between lawyers is probably more frequent and closer at this stage, dealing with the logistics of the process. Co-opertion can be enhanced. If a list of documents includes items which are unhelpful to a party's case, there has been a recognition of duties to the court and the legal system, as well as the client; this can re-kindle faith in lawyers' human nature. For all these reasons discovery can be a fruitful point to try mediation.

Some would argue that in cases of any complexity discovery is the first point at which mediation can sensibly take place. I think that is an extreme stance and is only arguable in rare cases. I am supported in this view by the London Common Law and Commercial Bar Association proposal of September 1990 which said:

> 'Our experience as practising trial lawyers is that it is unusual for the parties not to have seen and understood the significance of prejudicial documents very early on and it must be remembered that in the great majority of cases, the disclosure of relevant documents is achieved without order and on trust. In the result we propose that parties be invited to agree to 'core discovery' only prior to mediation'.

In fairness to the authors of this report they do go on to suggest that some may feel that full discovery is necessary in more complex cases, or even all.

The issue of discovery arose in two personal injury cases I mediated in 1990. Both cases reached mediation without discovery having been undertaken. In both instances the plaintiffs were young lads who had just left, or were about to leave, school when serious injuries occurred as a result of road traffic accidents. The areas of uncertainty and controversy centred on what their earnings would have been had they not been interrupted in post-school skill training. In the first case, the plaintiff's solicitor understood he was on fairly weak ground because neither the formal education (GCSE) nor the YTS report gave any indication that the plaintiff would otherwise have attained the level of technician, as was being asserted on his behalf. The solicitor had not found out what large companies were paying skilled fitters aged between 17 and 20 and decided not to continue the mediation, being uncertain about the precise size of this aspect of the claim. In the other case there were similar facts: the plaintiff hadn't worked in his late teens because, he said, of the injury. He had lost the opportunity to train for a particular career; again there had not been a full investigation into detail, nor full disclosure of documents relating to this part of the claim. The plaintiff's lawyer recognised certain weaknesses in the foundations of his argument – in fact that there was a poor school record and poor performance recently. He decided to use this head of claim as part of his negotiation strategy, but not to rely on it completely. At the same time, the defence were happy to assist in estimating the approximate loss of earnings in this area, had it been properly established, while professing their amusement that it should be put forward at all seriously! The final bargaining involved 'horse-trading' on a range of other issues as well and a deal was eventually struck. The parties had, in effect, decided that the whole exercise involved analysing the risks of continuing litigation. Looking at one aspect and accepting something short of precision in quantification did not prevent overall settlement because (a) this was only part of the negotiation, and (b) the argument itself was uncertain and some give-and-take was inevitable. The position is perhaps a bit different where the documentation goes to the heart of liability rather than causality and quantum, but even here I do not consider full discovery is necessarily vital, for the reasons set out in the proposal referred to above.

Another stage at which mediation may be appropriate is after exchange of statements – either expert or witness statements or both. Once again, there are arguments as to whether *exchange* is necessary for a successful mediation. On the whole it is helpful, but not necessarily vital, particularly if the mediator is knowledgeable about the subject matter of the dispute and the parties trust him enough to reveal portions of a report, or reports, in private session which then enables the mediator to ask cogent questions of the other side, without automatically revealing the expert's conclusions.

If any conclusion can be drawn from this look at the appropriate juncture for mediation, it is that clarification and information criteria suggest the process should take place at the end of an interlocutory stage, while cost-saving criteria indicate it should take place before the stage has commenced. In other words, mediate well before pleading, further and better particulars, and discovery starts or once it has been properly concluded. Applying this rule to the trial itself, mediate well before the court door and preferably before the delivery of the brief to counsel. Leave negotiations at trial to the face-to-face approach, but if the trial ends with the prospect of an appeal, consider mediation before everyone has become entrenched in the appeal process. It is of interest that the Courts and Legal Services Act 1990 encourages an 'appraisal' of the case at various stages of litigation. The aim is to encourage a quicker and more focussed case development. That appraisal should also consider ADR.

WHAT CASES ARE UNSUITABLE?

I have discussed a number of cases and situations where mediation is appropriate. When is it not appropriate? Obviously in those cases where settlement can be achieved face-to-face or by correspondence. Just as obviously, in those cases where there must be a court ruling, as in wardship cases and most criminal cases (although the concept of mediation in plea bargaining raises interesting issues).

There are those cases that one or other side wish to take to court, in order to set a precedent. These will normally be larger cases with corporate litigants. However, those very litigants may on occasion be reluctant to have an adverse precedent and in those situations mediation could be a suitable alternative to outright concessions.

There are also cases where it is clear from inter-party communication that both parties have offered their final settlement position. The trouble is that no one can be really sure that their final settlement position won't alter and it is wise to keep an eye on this from time to time. However, these are the cases where attitude precludes mediation.

Finally, there are cases which could be suitable but have not reached the point where meaningful discussions can take place. In most personal injury cases it takes months and sometimes years for a doctor to be able to give a final report; the injury needs to settle down. In cases involving property valuations and survey, reports need to be obtained. In complex financial cases accountants may take a long time to prepare a complete analysis.

HOW MEDIATION IS ARRANGED

Mediation can be arranged directly but it is more likely that agreement to mediate by all parties will be achieved by the intervention of a neutral agency or organisation such as IDR Europe Ltd, the British Academy of Experts, the Chartered Institute of Arbitrators or CEDR. These are currently the only organisations in the UK knowledgeable about ADR and with access to trained mediators and other ADR neutrals.

IDR Europe Ltd, through its association with ADR Net Ltd, has nearly one hundred lawyer mediators spread throughout England and Wales who come from a variety of large solicitor's practices. There are also some barristers on the IDR Panel and other professionals from insurance and construction. Further details should be obtained from them, CEDR, the British Academy of Experts or the CIA before deciding on which to use. These details will include: fees charged, experience and training of the mediators and the success rate in getting agreement to the mediation and subsequently the settlement rate.

Once selected, the first task of the agency is to approach the other party(s) to invite them to take part in the process. This will involve sending information material and following up with a telephone call and probably further communication to encourage the party to take part in the mediation. Sometimes this has proved difficult.

Lawyers and their clients are not familiar with ADR, let alone mediation; they confuse it with arbitration and are sometimes suspicious. English solicitors can resent an outside non-legal organisation 'interfering'. On one occasion IDR's case administrator got a curt 'If my client wants to settle she will tell me and we will do so in our own time' and the telephone was slammed down. It may be that as the process becomes more familiar and more popular there will be a lot more cases referred by both parties, but at the moment a key stage is seeking to get agreement to mediation.

IDR Europe Ltd have decided it is better to approach the solicitor (if there is one) for this agreement. This does then leave to the solicitor the job of persuading his client. IDR provide information and a video about the process and the ADR movement is addressing its arguments to industry, commerce and the individual as well as the legal profession. Nevertheless even if the lawyer thinks mediation is appropriate, he will probably still have some difficulty persuading his client. I deal with the client's perspective in a later chapter.

The next task is to select a mediator. The ADR agency will normally put forward several names who are suitable by reason of location and specialism. It is clearly important that all the parties feel comfortable with the person selected. In one case the mediator was felt unsuitable by the plaintiff since he came from the same city as the defendant's solicitors; the defendant also objected to the next name put forward on the ground that he was a civil engineer and more likely to sympathise with the plaintiff architect. I was the lucky beneficiary of this 'mediator vetting', though it was not an easy case.

I recommend that lawyers on both sides should pay attention to who the mediator is. Should (s)he be a lawyer or are there grounds for deliberately choosing a lay mediator? Is the case one where a particular expertise will help? How much experience has the mediator had and at what level of case? Can references be provided, particularly from parties to earlier mediations done by the chosen person? Everyone involved in ADR, from my experience to date, earnestly wants to maintain and improve standards but there will always be some who are better than others — although the ability to mediate won't necessarily be reflected in achievement in the mediator's main career.

The agency will then have to deal with costs, issues such as discovery necessary for the mediation and actually arranging the meeting, ensuring that all the necessary participants attend.

The trouble with mediation is that it is not a necessary stage in the development of a dispute, it costs money and does not automatically achieve a satisfactory result. The 'pennywise' approach is to disregard it and plough on with litigation or delay, whichever. But even the pennywise can strike a good deal. Although the norm is for each party to contribute equally towards the cost of the mediator and the agency administration costs, there are a number of litigants who consider that the advantages of settlement, made more likely by mediation, are such that they are prepared to pay all the costs – perhaps on the basis that they are likely to have to pay costs at the end of a trial, so why not do it earlier and more cheaply?

The costs are made up of three elements: *first*, the fees of the mediator, *secondly*, the administration charge of the agency and *thirdly*, the 'own costs', ie the legal and managerial costs of litigants attending a session.

Mediators charge according to their opportunity cost, in other words what they could be earning elsewhere. There may be some discount for a short, sharp and efficiently packaged job which yields a fee quickly, but the proper guide is the hourly rate of the professional who is selected as mediator. Mediations typically last from 4 hours to a complete day and IDR Europe Ltd operate on the basis that the mediator is guaranteed 5 hours' minimum remuneration. This allows for a small amount of preparation before-hand. In addition, the mediator will want his travel and other expenses and his travel time. Thus a mediator might charge £120 per hour and mediating in his home town would charge £600 for 5 hours.

Mediation companies in the United States charge a wide range of administration fees but in the UK for cases with over £50,000 in dispute, IDR charges £750 to include hire of rooms and all the administration of the process described above. Thus, the first two elements in this hypothetical case would amount to £1350 plus VAT. On top of this there may be some expenses.

The third element is the legal fees incurred by each side. Given that some preparation will be involved before-hand, the cost could well exceed that of the mediation. Nevertheless the total will not greatly exceed £3000 in all, including the legal fees of both sides.

This does not compare unfavourably with the costs of a day of trial with Counsel, solicitors and experts. Of course this is a simplistic comparison, since the whole aim is to save not only the costs of any trial days but also the whole arduous and expensive process of preparing for trial. Even if mediation is not successful in achieving an agreement, as I have stated elsewhere, the clarification and narrowing of issues can save a lot of time and money in later preparation of the litigation.

Of course, if litigation is being conducted with a tight budget, even these figures can be seen as totally off-putting and it may take some time before mediation becomes a standard feature in litigation at all levels. However, the Lord Chancellor's Department has been conducting an investigation into the efficiency of litigation and into the costs and benefits of the diferent litigation stages – pleadings, discovery etc. If mediation is seen as a stage in litigation, in the right cases, it will display a good performance. This suggests that in the right form and with proper safeguards against coercion, and misuse by 'cost running', mediation could well be useful in directing the use of legal aid funds in the most effective way. If this can cut short complex cases, then funds may be released for other cases and, hopefully, an expansion of the scope of the scheme.

Once costs have been ironed out and it is established whether they will be shared or borne in any event by one side – with the possible addition, say, in legal aid cases that the defendant will pay the Plaintiff's legal costs in any event – there remains the job, normally carried out by an agency, of ensuring all necessary documents are ready (if possible exchanged) and finalising details of time and place for the session.

Sometimes it will be necessary to hold up the mediation to ensure a report is ready, or that vital information is obtained. It may still be a good idea to agree in principle to mediate and the mere intervention of a third party, the administrator for the ADR agency, can speed up the progress of a file and stimulate fresh face-to-face negotiations. It is a mixed joy for IDR to have cases settle before mediation, since fees are not then charged. On the other hand, there is satisfaction from having been part of a positive process and undoubtedly goodwill is generated.

The meeting can take place anywhere but my experience suggests certain guidelines not to be lightly disregarded. First, it should be at a neutral place to avoid either side having the advantage of a 'home match'. Secondly, there should be a minimum comfort level. By this I mean enough rooms, enough chairs, pens, drinks, lavatories, coffee and sandwiches. I have done mediations in five star London hotels and in small offices. To some extent the background of the cases dictates the type of accommodation, but there is still a basic level below which the process suffers. I did one personal injury mediation at some small offices, and I had with me an 'observer' who was training to be a mediator. When the joint session finished and each side was ensconced in separate rooms, I discovered there were not enough chairs in both rooms for the observer and me. The shuttle from room to room was accompanied by shifting my chair from room to room too, with the observer nobly carrying it like some feudal or African servant. My dignity was not enhanced and it is fortunate that there was considerable good humour on both sides. On another occasion, again in the plaintiff's solicitor's offices, the whole process was delayed by the solicitor being interrupted constantly, having to deal with the rest of his work and even going off to court for an hour!

Thirdly, it is useful to have desks and telephones in the rooms used for private sessions since, unfortunately, and especially in multi-party cases, there will be longish stretches of time when the parties have to occupy themselves while the mediator is talking to someone else. It is useful to leave a private session asking the lawyers and litigants to consider this or that issue –

essentially getting them to ponder the weak points – but this does not normally take more than ten or fifteen minutes. Thereafter there is a risk of boredom.

During the first mediation I took part in on behalf of a client, he and I spent a lot of time playing pool in the hotel games room. On the whole this was not a good idea as it gave the impression to the other side that we were being flippant. However, there is no reason why lawyers and clients should not get on with other work during the fallow periods. I make a point of ensuring telephones are available for outside calls.

HOW TO PREPARE A CASE

'Shy and unready men are great betrayers of secrets; there are few wants more urgent for the moment than the want of something to say' – Sir Henry Taylor

The first precept is *know your case*. Fortunately, this does not mean quite the in-depth knowledge that is required to present a case at trial since there is no organisation of witnesses, careful analysis of procedure and the rules of evidence. It will, however, be necessary for the lawyer presenting his client's case at mediation to appreciate, and have considerable facility with, the key legal and factual issues. It is helpful, as this is a feature of mediation, for the strengths and weaknesses to be analysed, and even listed.

Commonly, the mediator asks each party, or his lawyer, to make a short opening statement. It is not a bad idea, at the outset of preparation, to produce an opening statement in written form. This will set out succinctly the facts and law. More detailed information and argument could be added at the end in the form of key letters and reports. This can then be checked with the client for accuracy and forms the basis of the presentation, both on liability and quantum.

Some mediation guides from the United States suggest that the opening statement, be it written or oral, should be the first move in the settlement process and should represent a settlement analysis. I don't agree with this approach for two main reasons. First, the opening half an hour of the mediation session is too early for any negotiation because the parties are getting used to the process, talking to the mediator and each other – premature settlement discussion can be harmful: phrases such as 'I won't settle for a penny less than fifty thousand pounds!' are a sure turn-off. Secondly, in this country the participants, lawyers and clients, are likely to come with an adversarial background and have been considering the case in the light of litigation in the High or County Court.

The opening statement is more useful to the mediator, and the other side, as a summary of the 'legal' case, with an assessment of the size of the 'legal' claim if necessary; everyone can see where the litigation stands and the mediation can start on a firm footing. That is not to say that anyone should be abusive or unpleasant and courtesy is very helpful at this point.

Having sent the draft opening statement to the client for approval, the solicitor should next meet the client to discuss the following:

(1) The mediation process, the mediation agreement and the agency procedures

(2) Plans for a negotiation strategy

(3) Who should attend and with what authority

(4) What part each should play.

(1) The mediation process

Considering what mediation is about is useful for both lawyer and client. It is sensible, for instance, to look at the mediator's role. He is not a mere messenger, shuttling back and forth with offers; therefore, it will be necessary to be flexible in your approach to how offers are dealt with. It is not always possible for the mediator to come back with a precise figure but he may indicate that there has been 'some movement' in response to an offer. The mediator knows more than each side alone and, if acting wisely, will gently manipulate the parties by floating proposals without disclosing what the other side is actually saying at a particular point. If you and your client appreciate this then your response will be more positive and conducive to settlement. It is also worth reminding the client that if the mediator starts asking tough questions ('Questioning is not the mode of conversation among gentlemen'), then although he may not be a gentleman he is not biased but is trying to bring both parties to a realistic appraisal of the case.

(2) A negotiation strategy

A negotiation strategy will begin to suggest itself with an assessment of the case carried out when preparing the opening statement. A settlement position on liability and quantum should be determined and the reason for those positions should be carefully analysed. This will enable a more rapid re-assessment as points are clarified at mediation and fresh facts and arguments are disclosed. As I have said earlier, negotiating positions change during the negotiation process.

It is important to decide, beforehand, what issues are going to be central, in order to react rapidly and perhaps score an advantage over a slower opponent.

With the client you will determine the actual figures, simplistically: *best position, acceptable, bottom line*. Wherever possible have objective verification to substantiate a stance or offer and, other factors apart, let the opposition have advance copies of schedules of figures and reports which will save time at mediation.

Sharpen up your best arguments and your responses to weaker points. Decide on your approach to the mediator since he is the vehicle for your arguments (for the most part) and the more he respects your approach the more likely it is that he or she will put your case effectively as the devil's advocate.

Lastly, decide what parts of your case you do not want to disclose to the other side, and what parts you do not even want to tell the mediator. As a mediator myself, I would prefer each party to have the utmost faith in me and disclose all. With everything disclosed to the mediator, so the argument goes, he is in the best position to push for the solution which is most likely to be acceptable to all. Even so, I am realistic enough to recognise that parties do not always trust me enough to disclose all *and*, like it or not, there is an element of 'persuading the mediator' in the process; all the more reason, some feel, for not revealing warts and other very confidential features.

It is difficult to be general about what, and what not, to disclose; so much depends upon individual circumstances.

I find it helpful as a mediator to see the opinion of Counsel upon which a party may be basing some or all of its arguments. Obviously, if litigation continues, it will be unhelpful for the other side to have read Counsel's opinion. On the other hand, it is probably wise to avoid the tendency to keep your ace up your sleeve too long. After all, with almost compulsory exchange of witness statements and fuller pleading of cases, favourable and unfavourable factors cannot be 'protected' too long in litigation nowadays. If disclosing something is likely to lead to a successful mediation, and an acceptable agreement, then it should be done. On the other hand, prudence dictates that some matters are best kept very close to the chest. I cannot draw from cases I have mediated to illustrate this point, since in those cases the participants retained these confidential cards, unrevealed. However, in a case I referred to mediation on behalf of a client, we had both decided at an early stage that taking the case to trial would be too expensive and damaging in terms of publicity. It would have been unwise to let even the mediator know this, since he would then have been unimpressed by arguments put forward that my client would call such and such a witness, and that his testimony would be this or that, knowing full well that there would not in any event be a trial. What about the ethics of misleading the mediator? That is for another volume!

(3) Who should attend

Who should attend is vital because the aim is to secure an agreement on the spot and this requires someone with sufficient authority representing the client. That person must either have intrinsic authority or be delegated with sufficient authority to settle within the decided range. Delay in contacting head office, or an agreement in principle subject to ratification the next day, can both jeopardise the process. In the context of an insurance defence, the claims manager should be there as well as the solicitor (or barrister). In some personal injury cases Counsel may not be necessary but if he is available at the end of a telephone this can be useful, particularly for the solicitor who is a little unsure of himself. Of course, it is a well known negotiating tactic for the negotiator to make sure that he has a limit on his authority, thus protecting himself from conceding too much. Conversely, the other side can be persuaded, in order to get the thing finished, to settle at a lower level than they would really like. This can be dangerous because the chosen limit may be below the bottom line of the other side, and the mediation will have been wasted. It is both sides who benefit from early settlement and if the above tactic defeats early agreement, then all the risks and costs of litigation are resurrected.

(4) What part each should play

What part each should play can be important. Lawyers tend to take control of their client's case and often rightly so. There can, however, be occasions for the client to shine. Mediation is an opportunity for the client who will make a good witness to convey that fact to the other side. Even if he is not such a good witness, it is a useful opportunity for the client's own case to be put forward rather than sanitised through legal pleading. This is particularly so in personal injury disputes. The defence, unless private investigators are employed, will only see the plaintiff at trial. Here is an opportunity to see injury or scarring and hear in his or her own words how the injury has affected the plaintiff. Delicacy is of course needed. On the whole litigation is male-orientated and I felt a little concerned at asking an attractive girl to show nasty scarring on her knee to a roomful of men in one case I did. Foreseeing problems like this, a lawyer might suggest his client bring along a friend or perhaps have a secretary take part in the joint session to overcome the difficulty.

In a multi-party construction dispute mediated by an IDR mediator, the factory owner plaintiff was getting frustrated by the slow progress. The mediator bought the parties back for a joint session, almost doubting himself that there would be any more movement. At this joint session, the plaintiff went round the table attacking each of the defendants and practically reducing one of the small sub-contractors to tears. He was 'venting' his frustration. The expression of emotion seemed to shake everyone out of a restricted mindset, the case developed momentum again and settled, albeit two days later. Here is an example of the value of getting a client to take part and reveal his feelings.

PRESENTING THE CASE

Lawyers are not normally shy, but by reason of work pressures can be unready (see quotation on page 52 from Sir Henry Taylor): hence they can be great betrayers of secrets. If, on the other hand, the case has been well prepared and the nature of the mediation process has been well understood, then presentation is not that difficult. In some ways it is easier than conducting a trial, because there are no problems with evidence or procedure and errors can more easily be corrected in the informal atmosphere of the private session. Then again, for all the assiduous preparation that may have been undertaken, the lawyer will need to be alert and flexible. He will need to be able to select the main issues that will lead to a satisfactory solution but at the same time protect his litigation strategy in case the session is not successful. At times he may need to re-focus the mediator's attention if red herrings are being pursued, but do so in an inoffensive way. He will need to take on board some of the skills of the mediator and in particular adopt a willingness to see both sides of the dispute, both in terms of legal analysis and also in terms of how the dispute is affecting the personalities. With corporate, as with individual litigants, managers and executives become personally involved with a dispute and an understanding of this can provide a key to settlement. An appreciation of the other side's legal analysis enables the lawyer to anticipate 'strong' arguments and provide effective responses more quickly.

Speaking from my experience as a mediator over the last year and a half, I value in a presenting lawyer the following attributes, in no particular order of preference: articulacy, a sense of humour, a genuine desire to settle, a sound knowledge of the law and procedure applicable to the case, a good understanding of the facts, a courteous approach to me and especially to the other side. I also value an understanding of the mediation process and a willingness to take part in it fully. This last requirement may take some time to develop.

CONCLUSIONS

Why should a lawyer be present? I raised this issue at the beginning of the chapter, discussed various arguments and stated that in my view the success rate of the IDR Europe cases (82 per cent) was in large part attributable to the presence of lawyers at those mediations. In the light of the foregoing discussion of the lawyer's tasks — selecting, preparing and presenting cases in particular — it is easier to see why this should be so.

First, lawyers are central in deciding on *strategy and tactics* for a mediation. Secondly, they ensure vigorous and relevant *presentation of the client's arguments*. The inarticulate client on his own can easily get side-tracked and needs a lawyer champion to re-direct the discussion when necessary. Thirdly, the lawyer *eases communication* both between the client and the mediator and the client and the other side. This communication points in both ways in that although he is there to support the client and interpret his case to the others, he is also there to interpret common sense emanating from the mediator. Thus, the lawyer driving home hard points to his own client is immensely useful to the mediator, who himself is treading a tightrope, being the devil's advocate but at the same time trying to develop trust and a relationship with the parties.

A lawyer who knows his client can be harder with him than the mediator. Finally, the lawyer, with his opposite number and the mediator (if legally qualified), will be important in dealing with *legal and procedural issues*. These crop up frequently since many mediations are done against the backdrop of a courtroom scene and the process leading up to trial. Issues of costs, payment into court, admissibility of evidence and so forth are potentially difficult and even if the mediator is a lawyer, he is specifically not taking part to advise either side and is, from my own experience, very happy to let the lawyers decide what is the correct legal interpretation of a situation.

So the lawyer is important. What then is in it for him?

First, in the right circumstances and with the right cases, mediation offers a fresh **service** to the client, a service that can produce quicker and therefore cheaper and less stressful results than litigation. If a case gets to litigation, then mediation is a useful tool in the contentious lawyer's tool-kit. Many firms of solicitors, both large and small, see litigation as a necessary evil, at best scraping along the bottom in terms of earning a profit. Certainly, some larger firms have specialised litigation departments and occasionally are entirely specialised in litigation, but by and large property and commercial law is seen as more profitable and therefore more attractive. Clients also generally look upon litigation as evil and not always necessary. One medium-sized provincial practice always advises clients to walk away if the sum in dispute is less than £50,000. I am informed that having lost a multi-million pound litigation, a large nationally-known company has decided that the costs of going to law are too high and is not referring cases under £500,000.

City firms of solicitors regularly use the £100,000 cut-off figure, below which full-scale litigation is uneconomic. The trouble is that even large companies can ill afford to throw away sums of this magnitude. Furthermore, executives become attached to their claims and are not happy to see them dropped on purely financial grounds. There is no reason why mediation should not be attempted in such cases so long as the basic requirement of 'willingness to try' is present on both sides. If such cases are mediated, then the lawyer from more expensive firms can still represent his clients economically and at the desired level of fee-earner, because mediation is so much quicker and cheaper than litigation. If the case does not settle, then of course a choice would have to be made.

A really positive grasping of the ADR nettle could do both lawyers and clients a lot of good. Clients will be impressed by earlier and more efficient claims settling and their satisfaction will be reflected in more instructions over a wider field of law. It is a feature of litigation that success can have a positive effect on client loyalty and referrals of third parties. It seems likely that successful use of mediation (and other ADR techniques) will have the same effect but magnified. This is because not only will the result be satisfactory, but the means of achieving it are directed towards involving the client in the process of getting agreement and are therefore directed towards satisfying him – which is one definition of service.

Secondly, mediation can have a beneficial effect on **fee income** without in any sense destroying the economics of the litigation department. This latter point is so because most litigation cases will still continue to be litigated in the traditional manner and many need to be so dealt with.

The beneficial effect on fee income arises in these main ways:

(1) Quicker income
(2) Easier to collect income
(3) 'Happier client' income.

I have already dealt with the last point above, but even when interim billing makes point (1) irrelevant, the client is a large solvent institution and point (2) is marginal, it is always valuable for a solicitor to please his client.

Costs are delivered earlier if mediation leads to settlement. The theoretical disadvantage is that all the fees that would have been earned in the later phases, including trial, will be lost. However, this argument depends upon the assumption that there are no other cases coming up to fill the gap. In reality, the likelihood is that the litigator has a lot of files demanding attention and thus there is no real loss. On the contrary, the quicker turnover yields better cash flow.

The argument then develops into the field of collectability. There is a view that litigation fees can be divided into three parts. The first part, or third, is the subject of an interim bill submitted at a time when lawyer and client are both still full of enthusiasm. The second interim bill is more difficult to collect. Then – there is the final bill and the client naturally wonders why he has to pick up this last third when even the losing party is usually relieved of a third of the costs payable by the absurdities of the taxing system.

If mediation cuts the case short, then the bill is submitted at a point when the costs are more easily collected. At a time when there are mutterings from the Lord Chancellor's Department about the high level of legal fees and the value added (or not) by different stages of litigation, there is some merit in having done a job which is unequivocally cost-effective.

Thirdly, mediation is **stimulating and frequently enjoyable**. This is not such an intangible benefit for lawyers as it might at first seem. The law is, after all, a profession and, to some, a vocation. Despite the understandable and laudable pressure on lawyers to be more business-like and efficient, earning money is only one part of a lawyer's job. It is also important for there to be job satisfaction and even job stimulation. There is a need to motivate staff in order to keep them and partners themselves can benefit from involvement with new ideas and new approaches to the law.

I have found myself looking at my own litigation files in a different light as a result of being caught up in ADR and a fresh approach to dispute resolution.

This is not to say that I am actually considering referring all of these files to mediation. In a large number, for a variety of reasons, it is not appropriate. However, the effort of trying to see the case as the other side sees it, the look at what leads lawyers and their clients to make concessions and the constant consideration of alternatives, which are all features of mediation, have made me more aware of the dynamics of settlement. I recently lost an Order 14 on behalf of my plaintiff client. However, the District Judge indicated this had been a proper summons and that he thought the plaintiff should succeed at trial. In the days before ADR I might just have ploughed on as vigorously as I could. On this occasion I wrote to the solicitors conducting the defence and reported the outcome, some days earlier than their agents. I also sent my list of documents and drew their attention to the complexities of discovery (for them) and therefore the considerable increase in costs that the defendants would now suffer. The letter had the effect I wanted and the solicitor rang me to discuss the case. I indicated my clients might make some concessions but he must put forward a concrete settlement proposal. There is nothing very profound in this and the solicitor might have telephoned without a letter. The point I make is that *I* started to look at things differently. A case is not an end in itself and if there is an opportunity for a sensible deal it should be taken.

What is wrong with mediation for a lawyer?

In its place not a lot, but there are potential problems to consider.

A first practical problem is that if it does not work, mediation has increased costs by a certain amount. The spin-off, though, can be an important clarification and narrowing of the issues.

There is a fear that mediation will replace arbitration and to those professionals who do a lot of arbitration this would affect their fees. I was interested to see this fear at work when IDR was referred a construction case by a large firm of solicitors; the other side were represented by a firm of construction experts with a multi-disciplinary approach but a vested interest in arbitration. They rejected mediation, on principle it appears. In practice, there is little chance of arbitration being supplanted and this does not appear to be a valid reason for opposing the growth of mediation.

Perhaps a more real fear is the notion that the client will see his lawyer in a new light and will respect him less. There are two factors at work here. First, the process aims to bring the resolution of the dispute back into the hands of the parties and this must therefore involve some loss of a lawyer's 'sovereignty'. Legal cases are known to take on a life of their own and, as with the cartoon cow, the plaintiff pulling the horns, the defendant the tail and the lawyer milking, our profession can be the principal beneficiary of a dispute. Mediation does tend to remove the lawyer from this central role, although for reasons I have pointed out he is still, normally, a very important part of the process. Secondly, the role of the lawyer at the session is not one of unambiguous adversarial advocacy. He is juggling with several roles if he is trying to be really effective in getting a solution. Professor Scott of Brimingham University refers to the need for 'advogotiators', in other words people who advocate and negotiate at one time. This is quite a mouthful. With the less imaginative client it can give rise to thoughts of 'He could have put that more strongly . . . ' and 'Whose side is he on anyway?' Before ADR becomes completely accepted I suspect that lawyers will have to select cases not only on the basis of criteria I have set out above, but also on the basis of the relationship they have with a client. I have one client, an industrial company, with an aggressive managing director who would think mediation a bit wet. It would have to be an absolutely perfect case for me to suggest mediation to this client.

To continue this theme, mediation presents problems for lawyers who like to rely upon the familiar comfort of well-used litigation procedures. In the example of two different approaches to discovery given on page 46, the first lawyer who wanted to adjourn the session to get more, and lean on 'discovery' information was not really at home with the process and his uncertainty may well have conveyed itself to his client.

Another problem is the question of what to reveal in the face of the impetus to disclose which can often be generated. Once the mediator has been told about certain confidential matters, there can be tacit pressure, later on, to disclose these matters to the other side in order to take the negotiations forward. This is not so much a problem for the sophisticated City litigation solicitor, but mediation is directed at a wide range of disputes and if one lawyer taking part is inexperienced or lacks confidence in litigation matters, then the risk is there that he will damage his client's case by being too open. But then, will such a lawyer necessarily do better for his client if the case goes on to trial – even if he does have his hand held by Counsel in the later stages?

So mediation can create problems and have disadvantages over more traditional methods of dispute resolution. On balance, however, it is a positive development for lawyers and I believe it will become a settled part of the legal scene. I feel that education about the process will overcome most of these problems. That education will be needed for the client, as well as the legal profession, and this is the theme of the next chapter.

CHAPTER 5

ADR (Mediation) from the Client's Point of View

'Civilisation is nothing else but the attempts to reduce force to being the last resort' − Ortega Y Gasset

The education of the client should not, but could, be difficult. The advantages of ADR mediation are manifold, the disadvantages slight: in the ADR jargon, 'there is nothing to lose' and 'preparation for ADR is also preparation for trial'. Therefore, the expenses of ADR are put to good use even if there is no settlement. Trial preparation is advanced, issues are narrowed and thoughts clarified.

The client, though, may initially see this as a new scheme by lawyers to add on a profitable stage − more work for more fees. Alternatively, he may feel that his lawyer has lost his bottle and wants to opt for an easy way out.

Putting the dispute back into the hands of the disputants can be seen by some as a 'cop out'. After all, some clients like to hand over the problem and let their lawyer to do the hard work, leaving to him not only the legal analysis and procedural control but the overall promotion of the case.

The most successful litigations I have been involved with have usually been for a client or clients who have formed part of a team with their lawyers and expert witnesses. The reason they have been vigorous and consistent members of that team, and vital to its success, are not hard to find. The client will almost invariably have a better feel for the facts than the lawyer (they are first and not second-hand); he will also have a better feel for what is in his best interests. On the other hand, he needs to be part of a team because he does not have the necessary objectivity, nor the legal and specialist skills; hence, he seeks professional help to conduct his case.

Therefore, from the client's point of view, one of the major advantages of mediation is that he not only takes an active role in preparing his case but is also an important part of the presentation team. I have dealt with this aspect in the previous chapter (page 55) under the subject of preparing the case. To reiterate, the client is there on the spot to make the commercial decision. He is also there to provide important facts and express his feelings, all of which can be helpful in reaching a settlement.

Putting the case in the hands of the lawyer and letting him get on with it, unaided, is by and large not in the client's best interests. Does he still have legitimate fears about ADR being a 'bolt-on' which increases fees and expenses and legitimate fears about his lawyer handing over responsibility for a successful result? There is no unequivocal answer to these objections save to say that in the right hands and with the right case, mediation need not give rise to these worries. Equally, with the wrong case and with the wrong lawyer, there could be grounds for concern.

To deal with the first of these matters, unnecessary increase in fees, the client has to be sure there is a reasonable prospect either of settling or getting movement before he commits himself to the process. To satisfy himself on this he will need to discuss the case carefully with his lawyer, consider the attitude of the other side, the general suitability of the case according to the guidelines set out in the previous chapter and his lawyer's assessment of the risks of litigation and the costs. I have already advocated that the lawyer should consult carefully with the client on these matters. At the same time the client should test his lawyer to see whether mediation, or some other ADR technique, is being put forward as a new gimmick, as something to do to avoid getting down to the arduous task of preparing for trial, or as a genuine attempt to get progress, having analysed the situation carefully. If it is either of the first two reasons, then the client ought to be very wary of investing his money in ADR. It could be that looked at objectively, the case is appropriate for mediation but if his lawyer's attitude is wrong then there are significant risks without commensurate advantages. For example, there is no longer as much strength in the argument that mediation preparation is valuable even if the case does not settle. If the lawyer has the wrong attitude, then he is unlikely to prepare properly. Furthermore, ill-prepared, he may make tactical mistakes and unwise concessions at the hearing. Unfortunately, it is possible to foresee a situation where mediation becomes a routine stage in a dispute akin to pleadings or discovery, an opportunity for the less scrupulous lawyer to increase his fees in what might be seen as an untaxing environment – if he does not try very hard. There is, after all, no judge to make a personal order for costs. The client should be on his guard against this and is entitled to be given a thoughtful justification for an attempt to mediate. He is entitled to far more than mere platitudes to the effect that it is a good idea.

The other fear raised is that during the mediation process for one reason or another, the lawyer abdicates responsibility or at least is perceived by the client to cease to be his champion. I have touched on this matter earlier in the book but it is important enough to come back to, this time looking at it from the client's point of view.

If the client has tested the position with his lawyer, as suggested above, then he should be able to determine whether his lawyer has suggested or gone along with an ADR initiative for the right or wrong motives. One of the latter could be the desire to get rid of an old and awkward file and to pass the job on to the mediator. But the desire to get rid of an awkward file does not necessarily mean that the lawyer is giving up and passing over responsibility. He may well genuinely believe that mediation is the best way forward and indeed there is a view that mediation is ideally suited for the file that has got bogged down. Some London firms have a system of 'skeleton transference' whereby at regular intervals they pass the old sleeping files on to other partners to bring them to life. Skeleton transference to the mediator is no bad idea. IDR Europe Ltd had a pilot project with London & Edinburgh Insurance Ltd in 1990, now developed into a full relationship. During this pilot project, a significant proportion of the cases referred by London & Edinburgh were old cases that for various reasons had become difficult to keep moving. Accordingly, the client should be sensitive to the thinking behind a referral to mediation and be slow to jump to the conclusion that the motivation is wrong.

Perhaps the more serious issue is the point that the methods of ADR and mediation involve a flexible approach that is not always strictly adversarial; therefore, some clients could *feel* their lawyers are not carrying out their functions properly, at least they are not carrying out their function in the expected manner. Without suggesting that there will not be instances of poor quality legal representation in ADR cases, this issue is primarily one of the need for the client to be educated about the subject and to understand what is involved, both in terms of the philosophy and the thinking behind each of the ADR techniques being used.

IDR Europe Ltd has considered in depth how to approach the question of educating the client, since this is also an integral part and of marketing ADR which is its essential commercial purpose. CEDR, a non-profit making company, requires its members to pledge to use ADR before litigating disputes between themselves. Both IDR and CEDR have given seminars aimed not only at the legal profession but also at the wider field of industrial and commercial clients. IDR has approached insurance companies indemnifying both commercial and personal policyholders, informing them about the existence and nature of the process. However, from the point of view of the client, these initiatives are primarily promotional and marketing endeavours of a general nature and on their own do not satisfy the need for a quite detailed understanding of the process.

IDR has come to the conclusion that the main effective way to educate the client is through the legal profession itself, in other words lawyers assisting in the education of their own clients. There are two specific mechanisms to carry this out. First, ADR Net Ltd, a company limited by guarantee, has been set up, consisting of some twenty firms of solicitors evenly spread throughout England, Wales and Scotland. Secondly, ADR Register has been set up. This is a directory of other firms of solicitors who are interested in considering and discussing ADR and mediation with their clients. They are provided with information about ADR, advice on how to select, prepare and present cases for mediation and local seminars for fee-earners and clients. Details of both these organisations can be found in Appendix 7.

ADR Net members will have fully-trained mediators available whose knowledge of the process will be central to the process of educating the firm's clients. Furthermore, a directory published by Waterlow Publishers called *A Director's Guide to ADR* has been written specifically for the commercial client. Indpendently, IDR will continue to develop initiatives in different market sectors and through Chambers of Commerce, trade organisations and professional bodies. CEDR and the British Academy of Experts and the Chartered Institute of Arbitrators will no doubt also continue to promote the subject.

Undoubtedly, these ventures have a commercial purpose, in the case of ADR Net and ADR Register to promote the ADR Net firms and to provide ADR Register firms with the ability to promote themselves as being knowledgeable about the practices of ADR. Nevertheless, they will also be important vehicles for the education of the client. What then is to be the content of this education?

Perhaps the starting point for the client is the following argument:

(1) ADR means Alternative Dispute Resolution. 'Alternative', that is, to litigation in particular.

(2) Litigation in this context means not only cases that reach trial but also litigation that is settled before or as it reaches the court steps.

(3) More than 90 per cent of such litigation settles, often after years of preparation, worry and expense.

(4) The initiation of litigation gives rise to an adversarial attitude: in the lawyer through his training; in both the lawyer and the client through the combative instinct in a 'fight' situation.

(5) The adversarial attitude itself generates extra legal work, delay and acrimony and in particular generates a lack of trust and poor communication.

(6) ADR seeks to speed up the settlement process and thereby save managerial and legal time and expense. To do this it aims to improve *communication* between the parties about what the dispute is really about.

(7) To develop better communication involves the creation of *trust*, but the adversarial attitude fuels distrust. Therefore, most ADR techniques have at their heart the blunting of the adversarial edge. Hence, a lawyer will not always be an aggressive champion.

If the client appreciates this argument he will be much happier about his lawyer refraining from 'tearing the other side to pieces', and instead, taking a more pragmatic approach. It is of note that in Roget's Thesaurus 'pragmatic' is juxtaposed between 'powerful' and 'utilitarian'. If the client sees his lawyer in this light he may understand the strength of the above argument.

The next point is the one about team work. I talked earlier about the need for a client to work as part of a team with his lawyers and experts. At its best the ADR approach includes another element in the team — the opponent. The better communication generated by a sufficient level of trust is greatly enhanced by considering the opponent as a member of the same team, all of whom are looking for the optimum solution, which is the easiest to achieve through a mutually beneficial outcome.

So these are the general precepts the client should take on board when looking at ADR. We should then look at some of the specific advantages on offer and finally the practical steps to take the case to mediation which have been looked at in the last chapter.

Some of the specific advantages of ADR for a client are set out briefly in the following list, in no particular order of importance (this list was prepared by an Australian ADR company, LEADR, and is designed for lawyers to educate their clients).

A. As fast as you want
ADR processes can be arranged within days or weeks rather than months or years, as can be the case in litigation (or arbitration). Mediation is normally over after one session and the norm is three to five hours. Even mini trials and private judging sessions are considered lengthy if they take more than three days.

B. Less expensive
Early settlement saves managerial time. The actual processes themselves cost less than litigation and arbitration.

C. Can walk out at any time
Unless the process is a court order, ADR is voluntary and therefore the parties are free to walk out at any time without interfering with their legal and procedural rights.

D. Confidential
The confidentiality of ADR means no publicity and no invocation of unwanted third parties such as competitors, regulatory agencies or the Inland Revenue.

E. No precedent
As with 'face to face' agreements, the confidentiality of ADR means there is no precedent. This can be important for clients who rely on a number of contracts of the same type or who have standard terms of business that affect their core business. An adverse result in court, even if no technical precedent is set, can create a welter of claims or defences and for this reason alone a case can be dropped.

F. Certainty of hearing date
The ability to choose the time, date and location of the hearing is a great advantage over the court system. The disadvantages of uncertainty about trial dates affect clients equally as much as lawyers and this aspect is important.

G. Maintenance of continuing relationship

Litigation and arbitration involve 'attriting' the other side (to borrow a horrible phrase from the American Military). ADR looks for solutions to satisfy the interests of all. Even if the final result is more detrimental to one side, the pragmatism of the process of achieving the settlement can maintain and even enhance relationships. This can be of particular importance during economic downturn since alternative clients or suppliers are not so easily found.

H. More remedies

ADR techniques offer a greater range of remedies than within the litigation system. Contracts can be re-negotiated, settlements can include face-saving concessions, and non-legal factors such as personal or business relationships can be considered. An illustration of this point is the mediation on page 111 of Appendix 5.

I. Lawyer control

Sometimes a client loses control of his lawyer. The lawyer takes over the case and becomes personally involved in the outcome. One remedy is to change solicitors. However, this is costly and gives the wrong signal to the other side. ADR can be a way of controlling the lawyer in a positive fashion.

J. A sign of strength to use ADR

The traditional, but unimaginative, view is that the party making the first offer or the first move to negotiate is the weaker party. ADR overcomes this bar or barrier to negotiation. First, an attempt to settle on advantageous terms is a sign of strength. It is an attempt to save costs and delay. Secondly, a willingness to trust the other side and talk through a problem rather than keep arguments in reserve is also a sign of strength. Thirdly, at the mediation, if that is the chosen process, the mediator can float settlement proposals without either side making that so-called weak first offer.

K. Complex technical issues

Under the present systems of litigation and arbitration the expert is frequently 'educated' to promote the client's case. This can be a problem if the judge rumbles him. ADR enables a truly neutral expert to be selected who can dispassionately advise and even suggest novel options previously not considered.

L. Elimination of the risks of uncertainty

Settlements in traditional dispute resolution are often pressured by the fear of uncertainty. The unpredictability of the result ('Which side of the bed did the judge get up on?') can lead to clients deciding to settle on relatively unfavourable terms. ADR enables the parties to control the settlement process to eliminate these risks and concentrate on the real issues between them.

Conclusions

There is no doubt that ADR can be of great use to the client. At the same time, it is not always appropriate and it is not the answer to all contentious issues facing the client. Accordingly, the client as well as his lawyers will have to select. He will have to choose which cases are right and he will have to be satisfied that his lawyer is both able to and willing to commit himself to the philosophy of ADR. This does not mean emasculation. The mediator is neutral not neutered. Equally, the lawyer does not need to be soft and indeed at times he needs to be tough on behalf of his client. However, he is negotiating in the context of a system that puts great importance on co-operation. He is therefore neither an out and out advocate, nor a mealy-mouthed conciliator.

Having satisfied himself that the case is right and that his lawyer is in the right frame of mind, the client also needs to make an adjustment to his own attitude towards the case. He needs to see the wood from the trees, in order to take the most advantage out of the ADR process. This means, primarily, understanding that both (or all) sides will be making concessions from their pre-mediation stated positions. An appreciation of this allows the client to plan his strategy very carefully, which is the best way of maximising the final result. The other factor to stress is that the client will get the best result by involving himself in the process of dispute resolution and the building of a *team* effort.

CHAPTER 6

How to be a Lawyer Mediator

'No man forgets his original trade: the rights of nations, and of kings sink into questions of grammar, if grammarians discuss them.' – Dr Johnson

A light-hearted list of the desirable qualities needed in a mediator was drawn up by an American mediator, William Simkin; he wrote in 1971 that the mediator should have:

(1) the patience of Job

(2) the sincerity and bulldog characteristics of the English

(3) the wit of the Irish

(4) the physical endurance of the marathon runner

(5) the jinking ability of a Welsh fly-half (Simkin was referring to half-backs)

(6) the guile of Machiavelli

(7) the personality-probing skills of a good psychiatrist

(8) the confidentiality of a mute

(9) the hide of a rhinoceros

(10) the wisdom of Solomon.

He continued with some more serious requirements, one of which was 'sufficient personal drive and ego, qualified by a willingness to be self-effacing'. Another American summed up this quality as 'an inoffensive presence'. Some lawyers, especially barristers, have an impressive presence. It is part of the stock-in-trade of the advocate to impose his personality upon the court. However, such people do not always have the ability to project their personality or their presence in an inoffensive way. They find it difficult to suppress their ego and to focus fully upon the problems of others. Winning a Court case can be achieved in a 'selfish mode'. Solving a conflict by mediation requires in addition some degree of 'self-effacing'.

There is of course no reason why a significant number of lawyers should not qualify, revealing inherent and acquired skills and abilities matching some or all of the qualities listed above. However, for lawyers (barristers and solicitors) to be effective mediators, they will have to recognise that they do not have an automatic right, by virtue of their legal skills, to dominate the process. Furthermore, they must recognise that mediation is not about procedural rules, about promoting conflict and adversarial combat to uncover the 'truth' of a matter. It is about attempting to uncover common ground with a view to problem-solving with a future orientation, rather than allocating blame and responsibility for the past.

This is not to say that lawyers will have to cast off their pin-stripe suits and take up sandals and gold earrings. Some of the more extreme exponents of ADR treat the subject as a semi-religion, describing experiences and ideas in mystical and ecstatic terms. Recognising this, IDR Europe Ltd has developed a term of mild criticism, 'He is behaving like a born-again mediator' to bring colleagues down to earth. Nevertheless, because their training is adversarial and directed towards historical analysis, lawyers in mediations must adjust their approach.

Unlike litigation and arbitration, the mediation is not primarily aimed at discovering what happened and then imposing a decision based solely on principles of law and justice. It is a *process* where lawyers/disputants invite a trained neutral to assist them to *negotiate*. Thus, a lawyer taking part must appreciate that he will not *win* a legal argument, and if the process ends in settlement, there may never be a clear statement as to who was right and what the 'true' legal position was. If he can make the necessary adjustments, an exciting and stimulating process is open to him. This different approach is emphasised by the distinction between process and content. That is the difference between *what* is done and the *way* that it is done. This point can perhaps be illustrated by an imaginary comparison between two identical cases, one that is mediated, the other litigated and then settled at the court door. If it is supposed that these are both partnership disputes, there would naturally be a considerable personal overlay involved. It is quite conceivable that the mediated case will result, objectively, in a lower payment for the outgoing partner, say, than the court-door settlement. However, proponents of mediation will argue that the consensual nature of the mediation process compared to the 'pressure/threat' situation outside the court, means that the first partner will be more satisfied with his settlement than the second. From this satisfaction, or lack of it, flow important future consequences in terms of acceptable relationships and manageable feelings about the whole episode.

THE SPECIAL VALUE OF A LAWYER MEDIATOR

All the cases so far referred to IDR Europe Ltd have either already reached litigation or are at least in the hands of lawyers. It seems likely that for the next few years a large proportion of ADR cases will have gone 'legal', that is until the concept spreads throughout industry and commerce and among individual members of society.

With the heavy legal element in the cases coming into ADR, it is very useful to have lawyer mediators taking part. There are three immediate reasons why this should be so. First, the knowledge of law and procedure will be extremely useful and may be necessary if only to make the participants comfortable. Secondly, it is likely that a lot of the lawyer mediators will have a specialisation or high degree of competence and experience in one or more particular areas of law. Thirdly, legal training and experience offer a good background for the ability to analyse a situation swiftly, which is a vital feature of the mediator's task.

Early mediations carried out in this country by IDR Europe in both personal injury and 'commercial' cases used non-lawyer mediators. Whilst these were largely successful (sometimes settlement came after further post-mediation negotiation), it was later decided that in cases where proceedings have actually been issued, wherever possible a lawyer mediator should be selected. This was primarily in the light of the first point above. It became clear that during the mediation process, sufficient points of legal and procedural importance arose to bring about this change of policy. Furthermore, it was discovered that mediator specialism was helpful.

Thus, when the lay mediator had to ask the meaning of this or that procedure and the likely impact of the judge's decision on costs, he was calling into question the professionalism of the mediation. Conversely, when the mediator could speak confidently and even authoritatively about particular areas – for example the notoriously difficult (to quantify) *Smith v. Manchester* head of damages in personal injury claims, or the meaning of a 'Tomlin' Order – then he is encouraging confidence in the process and in his ability to guide the negotiation to a satisfactory and perhaps even fair result.

In many ways this is a shame because non-lawyers can really break the mould and introduce a totally fresh approach to dispute resolution. I have a lurking fear that unconsciously lawyers could lead mediation astray. An easy way for this to happen is for there to be an automatic referral of cases to undertrained and untalented mediators or conciliators in a court-annexed scheme that has not been carefully thought out. In this situation, mediation will become just another step in the litigation process and familiarity could breed contempt. A more serious fear is that lawyers will alter the emphasis of mediation. They will make it a useful adjunct to the preparation for trial, making use of the clarification and narrowing-of-issues aspect, losing sight of the more revolutionary ability of the process really to bring about a change of attitude in other parties to their mutual benefit. The answer to these fears may lie in the wide range of matters that are suitable for mediation (see Chapter 2). There will be many cases that come to ADR early enough for there to be no particular need for a lawyer mediator. There will also be many cases where lawyer-experience and knowledge will be appropriate and even necessary. I hope that the advantages of having a specialist mediator (contrast this with the random allocation of judges in most litigation cases) will not prevent lawyer mediators covering a wide range of disputes in order to broaden their vision of the dispute resolution field and keep up their enthusiasm. Orthodoxy and convention could deal the subject a heavy blow.

PARTICULAR SKILLS TO DEVELOP

The skills or qualities listed at the beginning of this chapter can now be looked at in greater detail.

The patience of Job

This is sometimes called 'attending' and it involves demonstrating verbally, and non-verbally, that the mediator is attentive to the participants and is interested in what they have to say. A mediator should sit squarely, establishing and maintaining eye contact with all key participants, as appropriate. He should avoid distracting behaviour. To help in this the mediator will aim to sit at the head of a table with the parties on either side of him. Preferably this should be a round table to avoid the image of confrontation − sitting opposite each other. During one mediation I did there were several observers. This didn't matter as there were quite a few people at the session anyway. However, I began to notice that the lawyer for one of the parties kept looking over my shoulder. Quite simply one of the observers was a little bored and was fiddling in a frustrating way. This was easily rectified by shifting positions. It does, though, illustrate that concentration is required by all participants.

The jinking ability of a fly-half

This facility is very useful in what the ADR jargon calls 'responding'. The mediator's response to statements made to him must accurately reflect the feelings expressed by a party or his lawyer and the response must contain accurate and relevant content in relation to those feelings. The trouble is that each party will be on a different emotional and possibly intellectual plane. Hence the need to jink, since what is an appropriate response for one may not be for the other. I should explain that rugby fly-halves jink by elusively changing pace and direction in order to dodge opponents ('difficulties' for the mediator).

In the personal injury cases I have done, the claims manager and his solicitor, for the defence, have been analytical, calm and doing a job of work. The injured party and his or her lawyer have naturally been more emotive and, occasionally, upset about the case. This has called for different mediator responses in different private sessions. It should be added that this jinking may seem somewhat manipulative. It probably is, in the sense of influencing the process. It is not manipulative in the sense of persuading someone to do something they do not want to do, or something that is not in their best interests. After all, the mediator must build up trust to enhance communication and first he must build up trust between himself and the parties; responding properly is a useful though demanding way of doing this.

The physical endurance of a marathon runner

I find mediations exciting, stimulating, challenging and very tiring. This could simply be because they are still new, but I suspect it is something more. What I think is so tiring and demanding of endurance is the constant to-ing and fro-ing between respective points of view. A judge may enquire into the inner thoughts of a litigant (or witness) but usually only to elicit evidence. A mediator tries to understand these inner thoughts, tries to empathise, in order to discover what is the best and most practical way in which to bring about a settlement. The mediator is trying to find out what those feelings really are, the judge or arbitrator can stop (usually) when the evidence has come out. Added to this the mediator still has to handle the issues in an analytical way and keep on top of the changes in the negotiating stances that often occur. After a long mediation I find it takes at least twenty-four hours before I can get back into a fully operational state.

The guile of Machiavelli

Machiavelli was rather maligned by historians of his period. The term 'machiavellian' has connotations of underhand behaviour, perhaps even evil behaviour. It seems the better view is that he was an exponent of the art and science of diplomacy and, living as he did in war-torn Italy, abounding with intrigue, he started out as a man of peace exhibiting a lot of common sense. It could be said he was an early ADR practitioner.

The mediator uses machiavellian guile in a variety of ways. He uses it to disguise the critical direction of his *questioning*, which has the aim of bringing a party to a more realistic view of his case. He uses it to *re-frame* messages and statements from the other side in a non-judgmental way to

(1) emphasise positive aims
(2) emphasise common ground
(3) remove allegations of fault and blame
(4) identify underlying needs, and
(5) expand to a fuller meaning, clarifying assumptions and implications.

He also uses this guile to *re-focus*; this involves recognising the significance of side-issues, then setting them aside and re-directing attention and discussion back to the central issue(s).

I make a point of telling each side early on that being the devil's advocate it can seem at times as if I am attacking them personally. I stress that the same process is going on with the other side and I am not showing bias or prejudice. However, it is not enough to make this statement and then go in with all guns blazing. Throughout the session the mediator must measure the tone and pitch of his language and this includes his body language — position, gestures and facial expressions.

By 'measuring' his verbal and non-verbal communication the mediator is by no means simply bringing everything down to a calm, matter-of-fact level, although this can be useful. It is a question of reacting in an appropriate fashion. Thus, if a party is speaking fast and with a slightly raised voice, then the mediator should consider following suit in order to get on to the same level of communication and then to lead the conversation in the required direction. Other options for the mediator in this situation are to talk in a calm quiet fashion or to take a firm parent-like stance. The risk of the former is that the contrast between the mediator and the emotional party will enrage the latter and disrupt communication. The risk of a parent-like attitude is similar.

During one mediation I described in Chapter 2, a colleague and I saw the unrepresented surveyor on his own a number of times. He was adamant that he was not at fault and was stubbornly vociferous in representing that position to us. One approach we adopted was to speak down to him stressing the irrationality of his position. The tone and speed of our language was different from his, it was superior and at a different tempo. Later we each saw him separately and, independently of each other, both got through to him much more effectively, so much so that he made just enough concessions to allow a settlement. During these later meetings I and my colleague, Andrew Floyer Acland (author of *A sudden outbreak of common sense; Managing conflict through mediation* — Hutchinson Business Books) actually measured our responses to the man. First, we argued with him at his level and speed. We traded arguments, using forceful language and in a jocular way. Then, when both sides had exhausted the first flush of argument we reduced the speed and volume of the discussion and gradually bought him into a more reflective frame of mind. It was not easy and from time to time his emotion could flare up again, but we had by then established enough rapport to bring him back quickly.

I can foresee allegations of 'manipulation' being raised once more. Again, the defence is that although the mediators were influencing the content and directions of the discussion they were not manipulating the surveyor in the sense of tricking him into concessions on the basis of false information or indeed false arguments. Save in unusual circumstances, where the mediator expresses his own opinion, all that he is doing is conveying the opposition argument to the other side, albeit expressed in his own way.

I have to concede, nevertheless, that there is a theoretical risk, particularly with an unrepresented party, that a forceful or very articulate mediator could so influence a party's perception of the case that he settles on disadvantageous terms. But that begs the question: 'disadvantageous compared with what?' Perhaps disadvantageous compared with what a court could theoretically order but (a) most cases do not get to court but settle face to face, (b) in a face-to-face settlement it is more likely than not that the other side would be even more disingenuous than the mediator in this hypothetical situation, and (c) there is the residual right to set aside the settlement or rectify the agreement if the facts have been so badly misrepresented as to justify an application to the court.

Certainly, however, mediators must use their power and influence wisely and ethically which is where Simkin's final quality – the wisdom of Solomon – is so important.

The personality-probing skills of a good psychiatrist

A lot of the literature on ADR and mediation places emphasis on the analysis of human behaviour and personality types. There are endless variants but it is interesting that the analysis usually starts with four basic elements. Traditionally these were earth, air, fire and water; alternatively, blood, phlegm, choler and melancholy. IDR Europe has a training manual referring to:
- pragmatics or rulers
- extroverts or entertainers
- amiables or relaters
- analyticals.

Andrew Floyer Acland in his excellent book (see page 73) talks about:
- *Bulldozing*. Types who are goal-orientated, power hungry, aggressive people-users
- *Cycling*. Types who are relationship-orientated, create power through relationships, assertive, aggressive and enthusiastic, with leadership and manipulative characteristics
- *Helicoptering*. These are types who are goal-orientated, analytical; power is invested in technical expertise and intellect, they are passive/assertive and are not very interested in people
- *Rambling*. These are types who are relationship-orientated and power-averse. They are passive, warm and human.

Acland makes the valid point that no one individual fits neatly into one category. He therefore draws a map which he calls the behaviour map.

People move about this map but normally within adjacent 90° quadrants.

The value of all this analysis is to assist the mediator in recognising the sort of person he is dealing with and then to adjust his own style and behaviour to match. This enables rapport to develop and communication follows that.

THE BEHAVIOUR MAP

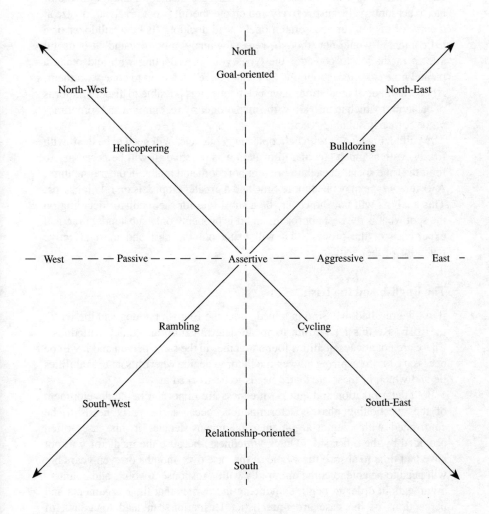

Ideally, the mediator should naturally find himself at the centre of the map and be able and willing to move into each quadrant to carry out this 'matching'.

I find the whole approach of limited practical value. This is because things happen swiftly and in unexpected ways during a mediation and the mediator has to act intuitively, instinctively and on the spot. It is not practical to gaze at a party or his lawyer and scratch one's head deciding 'Is he a bulldozer or a helicopter?' I would not, though, reject the analysis out of hand. It is useful after a mediation to consider the types you were dealing with and make a mental note of different options that could have been used to cope with them. After a number of mediations have been done, it is possible to discern patterns of behaviour which in turn allow the mediator early recognition and sometimes scope for early suitable reaction.

A bulldozing lawyer with helicoptering tendencies will need to be dealt with firmly, with as much tact and information as possible. It will be necessary to limit the time spent on each to prevent boredom and maintain the momentum. A different type may need more time and a greater emphasis on relationships. This analysis will not, however, be a substitute for the mediator deciding on the spot what is the best approach, and it is probably only substantial practical experience of the process that will bring out the best and most effective reactions of the mediator.

The English and the Irish

It will be recalled that Simkin talked about the English bulldog and the wit of the Irish. By this I take him to mean determination and quick-wittedness. These are not always qualities found together in the same person and it will be necessary for the aspiring lawyer-mediator to decide where his natural abilities lie and which of these attributes needs to be worked at.

Both determination and quick-wittedness are important in the development of the questioning phase. Determination, because the party needs to be confronted with counter-arguments and inconsistencies in his case, often provided by the other side. Quick-wittedness, because the mediator will not have had time to absorb the whole of the case over months or even years but will need to be able to come up rapidly with a response to points and counter-arguments in order to begin convincing the parties that their arguments and perceptions of the case are unrealistic. Hesitation can lead to a lack of credibility and an undermining of the mediator's authority.

Determination is also important in the negotiating phases of the process and particularly in the closing stages. The idea is to concentrate and telescope months of desultory communication to achieve a speedy result. It can be done in as little as two hours, even with fairly complex cases. However it can also take a lot longer. It is when the session has lasted 6 hours, non-stop, that determination becomes very useful. A feeling can creep in that everything has been tried and it is time to pack up. During one mediation I did the lawyer who sat in as an observer/trainee mediator said to me in the corridor of the hotel where we were operating that he felt there was no chance of settlement — the parties were too far apart. Having done a number of mediations, I had a feeling that this was not the case, particularly because no one had started making the sort of intention movements (rubbing hands on clothes, picking up pens etc) indicating they wanted to leave, and so I pressed on. About an hour later further movement occurred and eventually the case settled. At no point did I bully or cajole anyone to stay. On the other hand I just kept going. Equally, a construction mediation I did a few weeks earlier terminated after only two and a half hours. Here one of the parties began 'reverse-negotiating' — in other words taking concessions off the table as the process developed. Despite the obvious desire of the other side to settle, they could not stomach this approach and it was clear everyone was wasting their time.

The hide of a rhinoceros

It is a paradox that a mediator needs to be sensitive but at the same time be thick-skinned. Clearly he needs to be sensitive to pick up not only facts and arguments but also to detect deeper feelings and needs. There are at least five psychological issues that arise during mediation, all of which can pose problems for the mediator:

(1) Isolation
Most of the mediator's work is done in isolation from colleagues and from an established system of rules. He is on his own. This isolation does give him independence and considerable discretion but he does not have the support, reassurance and understanding of colleagues and can be treated as an interloper in the affairs of others.

(2) Helper role
The mediator is like other helping professionals in that he lacks the direct power to make things happen. He is limited to facilitating and encouraging things to happen. It is the parties themselves who have the final decision and must live with the results. Words like 'vicarious' and 'proxy' spring to mind and even, 'They killed the messenger . . . '

(3) Limited positive feedback
It is a feature of the process that if there is settlement and any congratulating to be done, then it is done between the parties. If there is failure to settle or the mediator fails to meet the parties' expectations, then there is more likely to be comment which will be adverse. Mediators have this in common, to some

extent, with barristers. A conference with Counsel may clear up a lot of problems but he may never hear of the case again. A difficult case keeps popping up like a bad penny.

(4) Confidential information
The absolute requirement of confidentiality limits the very human need to talk about the issues with other people. This can cause stress arising from the need to be careful in avoiding a slip whilst at the same time appearing natural and at ease with both parties.

(5) A filtered reaction is required
A related point is that the spontaneous give-and-take of conversation must be filtered to avoid saying anything which makes settlement more difficult. The emotive language of one side has to be sanitised to distinguish between the progress which is developing and the prejudice that can be detrimental.

In my experience, none of these problems is that severe. Difficulties lessen over time, with practice and a little awareness. The mediator should not expect to be liked or even thanked. If he has succeeded, it may be because he has asked some tough questions and brought both sides down to a realistic position. With hindsight, they may feel gratitude; on the day they have probably both had to make significant compromises and may not always be best pleased.

QUESTIONING TECHNIQUES

I make no apology for returning again to the topic of questions. If the private session represents the engine-room of the mediation process, then questions are the fuel for the engine and the lubricating oil too. Some of the main purposes of questioning are:

- To get facts/opinions about the case
- To check your understanding
- To channel the parties' thinking
- To get them thinking realistically
- To help them think constructively

The questions used should be *open* or *direct* questions.

Open questions get people talking and open up new areas of discussion. They should be phrased: 'How do you feel about . . . ?' and 'What are your views . . . ?' They should not be phrased: 'Will you . . . ?' or 'Can you . . .?' or 'Do you . . . ?' These closed questions will generate a yes/no answer and the dialogue will dry up. Direct questions are used to probe into particular areas and elicit specific facts.

The informality of mediation greatly assists the creation of a relaxed atmosphere and the mediator must try to avoid destroying this when interviewing the parties. The trick is to use a gentle conversational tone whilst at the same time asking tough questions which will make them think.

Although the mediator should not side with either party, he should listen actively to the responses to his questions. This involves leaning forward slightly, keeping good eye contact and nodding occasionally, perhaps with a 'uh huh' from time to time. If he indicates that he has understood what they are saying and what their point of view is, then he is in a better position to influence them and to stimulate further thinking and discussion. It can be useful to paraphrase: 'If I've understood you correctly, you are saying . . . '. This emphasises that one is listening actively but can also progress the discussion as the 'playback' may lead to a better definition of the problem or further thoughts.

Questions should be framed carefully. They should be short, relevant and single-barrelled. The words used should come easily and be understood easily. The questioning should be smooth and natural. It is a mistake to go in with a list of questions that simply must be asked. This is the beauty of not having a fully comprehensive approach to each and every detail of the case.

The following questions can be useful in dealing with both sides:

- What are the strengths of your case?
- What are the weak or limiting factors?
- What is the objective value of your case?
- What is the likely outcome before a Judge?
- What will the costs amount to at the end of trial?
- What do you think the other side would be willing to do to settle the case?
- What would you be prepared to do to settle?
- What would you be prepared to do to settle today?

These questions arise at different stages of the mediation and, as stressed earlier, it is unwise to press for a settlement strategy before communications have been built up and devil's advocacy has, hopefully, led to a more realistic appraisal. It is interesting to see how a series of questions on the objective valuation of a claim or counter-claim can cause a second look not only at quantum but the underlying thinking behind the claim. This is particularly the case in personal injury mediations and in the area of future loss of earnings, what jobs might have been obtained but for the injury and so on.

In the area of personal and partnership disputes, questioning can successfully reveal incorrect *assumptions* upon which conflict is often based.

The following diagram illustrates how assumptions are formed:

Intention	**Action**	**Effect (feeling)**
(private)	(public)	(private)

Intentions are often private, **actions** public, **effects** or results can again often be private. I mediated a case involving three partners in a professional firm. Two of the partners were in one part of a large office block and the third, in a different section of the business, in another office on a different floor. The two contacted the landlords with a view to leasing a further suite of offices immediately adjoining their existing offices. This action (public) gave rise to feelings of irritation and resentment in the third partner. Other problems arose and it looked as if the partnership was going to split up. The mediation was swiftly arranged to see if anything could be done to reconcile the parties.

During the early private sessions it became clear that there had been a lot of vague conversation about these new offices, but nothing definite. Partners A and B had finally decided to take the offices for expansion of their division. Partner C thought the intention was to close his offices and bring him up next to A and B's offices. He was against this on practical and personal grounds and so became upset. He had then failed to communicate clearly with A and B over the development of their plans and things went from bad to worse.

The mediation cleared up a number of wrong assumptions: first, C's assumption that the offices were to be taken on solely to move his section; and secondly, A and B's assumption that C was jealous of their expansion plans. In view of other underlying problems, it was not possible to reconcile the partners but the mediation did provide a forum for a co-operative division of assets. Clarification of the assumptions restored civility to the arrangements.

Some useful techniques

'Silence is the unbearable repartee' – G. K. Chesterton

The use of silence is something lawyers will have to learn, but will be attracted to once they have seen its power. I recall an early mediation I did whilst I was still learning. One of the parties, a businessman, was seen on his own and the meeting covered the different options available and the effect each would have on the financial settlement that was being sought. My natural instinct was to keep asking questions, probing into areas that I thought this man had overlooked, at the same time pointing out weaknesses in some of his assumptions. At the back of my mind there was a judge or master/district judge sitting before me with an acute forensic mind weighing up the answers, and creating some legal sense out of the exercise. In reality, I had before me a legally unsophisticated businessman who was getting more and more confused, and was not addressing the key issues. Outside in the corridor the colleague who was mediating the case gently chided me and told me to let points sink in. 'Let him make his mind up, don't give him the opportunity to get off the hook by going down other avenues'. From then on if I became too enthusiastic the mediator unobtrusively raised his head, indicating silence was called for.

This use of silence is not only a matter of courtesy to people who may not be at home with complex arguments and legal concepts and therefore need some time to absorb them. It also allows a hard point to sink in deeply. During this mediation there was another occasion, with the other party, when I noticed a full twelve minutes without a word being said by anyone. The man was formulating his first offer, his opening position. To have had a dialogue or series of questions at that point would have let him raise arguments justifying a lower offer. He could have 'hidden' behind words and positions. As it was we let him come up with the proposal unaided and he had to feel happy, on his own, that it was a reasonable stance to take. At this point I should add a word of caution: the mediator should be aware of turning a 'pregnant pause' into an 'embarrassing silence'. If the party really is out of ideas, there is no point in wasting time and irritating people in the process.

Of course the use of silence is a technique used in negotiation. I quoted earlier in this book the phrase that 'Shy and unready men are great betrayers of secrets . . . '. How much easier it is to get these secrets/positions disclosed by simply keeping quiet. The pressure to say something becomes unbearable and the chances are that progress can be made. With the better prepared it is still a valuable technique but may not bring about such immediate results.

Another technique is to encourage the parties to look at the case through the eyes of another person, usually an expert present at the mediation, although occasionally it might be through the eyes of the mediator himself. In some of the mediations I have done accountants have taken part. Usually they have prepared and disclosed reports. However, it is one thing to have a written report and another to hear opinions directly. There is another side to this technique: in a mediation done in September 1991, I brought the accountant into the private session with the other side. He heard the defendant and his lawyer discuss the case from their point of view in the less formal but still forceful atmosphere of a caucus. He then went back to the plaintiff and his lawyer. I have no doubt that he conveyed arguments in a very effective way. The case settled at a sum that reflected a significant shift from this accountant's initial report.

CHAPTER 7

Threat or Opportunity?

This chapter's title, and the rest of the book, operate on the assumption that ADR is here to stay. Clearly the movement will provide neither threat nor opportunity if it fades away like skate-boarding or, for the older generation, hoola-hoops. A number of signs, however, suggest this will not be the case. In the first place, the processes have grown and multiplied across the Atlantic to the point where enterprise capital in excess of $20 million has been raised by a grouping of ex-judges providing high-level mediations and mini-trials. Secondly, a number of substantial and influential organisations have been formed over here to promote ADR; these include CEDR and ADR Net, both of whom have member firms from amongst the largest legal practices in the country. Thirdly, the Law Society has described ADR, together with financial services, as one of the growth areas for solicitors in the coming decade.

Given, therefore, that ADR has a place in the legal system, is it going to be a threat or an opportunity for the legal profession, and in particular, solicitors? Is it going to become another bugbear for lawyers, like licensed conveyancing or banks doing probate? Or will it be a new source of work for professionals and, additionally, a way for them to give a better service to their clients? My feelings, unsurprisingly, are positive. However there are fears amongst some lawyers that the movement is not wholly good news. Some of these fears may have a basis in fact and I propose to examine them below.

The threat

The first fear is that in some way 'alternative' means 'alternative to lawyers'. Indeed the movement developed originally, in the United States, as a protest at the adversarial system and lawyers were kept away. Inevitably, however, lawyers took over the differing processes and are now dominant within the movement. ADR involves looking at strengths and weaknesses and analysing risks. In a wide variety of cases these are legal strengths and weaknesses and the risks of proceding to court. A lawyer must be in the best position to carry out these functions, both as a mediator and as presenter of his client's case. This is not to say that non-lawyers have no place; it is my view that the alteration of mindest that is needed to develop a good lawyer into a good mediator can best be learned by seeing an imaginative non-lawyer at work. Mediator skills involve a lot more than legal ability, but this does form the basis of what is needed in those cases with a legal element.

So far, the practice has been for ADR agencies, both abroad and at home, to recommend in clear and strong terms that unrepresented parties ought to take legal advice and should bring a lawyer with them to the mediation session. The IDR Europe Ltd Agreement to Mediate (Appendix 3) devotes most of one clause to stressing the need for legal advice, and also that the mediator is not acting as an adviser or a lawyer. It seems likely, therefore, that this first fear has little foundation. There may be community mediation programmes that exclude solicitors. There may be specially designed schemes which deal with the parties over the telephone to save cost. However, the development of ADR in those fields where lawyers already practise litigation and arbitration will not mean less work for lawyers but, simply, different work.

The second fear is that fees will suffer. The argument goes that if all these cases settle so much earlier, then the legal costs that are saved will be lost to the profession. There is some strength in this argument. After all, it is one of the points stressed by people advocating the use of ADR that less time amounts to less cost. Nevertheless, if one looks at the profile of a litigation solicitor's filing cabinet, the matter is not quite so straightforward. There will be many cases that are simply not suitable for mediation or any other such process. Either they are not ready — there has not been exchange of reports or discovery — or the attitude of the litigants is such as to preclude ADR. These cases will continue to generate fee income in the normal way. Of those cases that may be suitable for ADR, one may safely assume that 90 per cent will settle before trial in any event. Thus, the comparison is between earlier ADR settlement and later face-to-face agreement. The fees for trial should not come into the analysis.

The early settlement of those suitable cases is not by any means detrimental to the solicitor's cash flow. A speedy resolution means early settlement of the bill. Protracted negotiations can mean long delays in payment. Early resolution also means that the solicitor can get on with other cases. At the moment litigation work is abundant, and has normally been widespread. The solicitor will therefore have a number of satisfied clients: the litigant whose case has settled, and the clients whose cases are moving along faster because they are closer to the head of the queue. The lower fees from the mediated case are matched by the fees from other cases, with the added bonus of better-satisfied clients. Furthermore, if the solicitor becomes adept at presenting cases at mediation on behalf of the client, then he will be making good income for concentrated chunks of time, rather than half an hour here and there.

A third area of fear is perhaps more complex. This is the fear that by taking part in the ADR process, the lawyer becomes emasculated. That is to say that he ceases to be seen by his client as unequivocally his champion. Normally a client will expect his legal representative to advocate his case for him as vigorously as possible. In the mediation session the lawyer has to consider what the aim is. There is no real value in theatrically advocating to the mediator in the hope of convincing him of the truth of the case. The mediator is much more interested in the issues, the strengths and weaknesses and the party's interests. He is not there to decide. Accordingly, the presenting lawyer may well do better to adopt a less adversarial approach. The better line could be to discuss and analyse, the goal being a realistic settlement. The risk is, however, that along the way the client begins to wonder on whose side his lawyer is. I have already described lawyer presenters as 'advogotiators' – whatever this beast is, he will have to consider what effect he has on his client.

This issue arose in a mediation between two construction companies. The main contractor was refusing to pay one of the sub-contractors, alleging delay and poor workmanship. There was some merit in this counterclaim, but the sub-contractor appeared to have a case for a substantial payment. The main contractor's lawyer was an intelligent man and a good lawyer. He was aware of a number of arguments, factual and legal, that could lead to a defeat in court. Nevertheless, the client was taking a very tough stance. It was clear that the lawyer was of the view that the risks entailed in further litigation made settlement desirable. The client would not go beyond a figure which was far too low to reach a settlement. He was reckoning on the other side being unwilling to take the case to court. It was clear to me that the lawyer wanted to advance the negotiations but at the same time, he was concerned not to show weakness in front of his client. The talks foundered, but I believe they might have succeeded had the lawyer felt able to emphasise the legal risks more vigorously.

There is no easy answer to this problem. Naturally, the fear will vary according to the individual and his relationship with his client. Additionally, it might be felt that in agreeing to mediate, the client is already persuaded by the merits of discussion rather than war. This doesn't always appear to be the case. People negotiate 'on their feet' and this can require a rapid adjustment by the lawyer, in order to fall in line with a new tough stance. At the same time, he is still trying to manage the relationship with the mediator. Persuasion is best pursued through reasonable and rational argument in this situation. Hence the lawyer-presenter's dilemma. He needs to maintain the respect of the client and the mediator, but each may be looking for different qualities.

There are a number of developments which will reduce the seriousness of the 'weakness argument'. In the first place, as the ADR processes become better known, clients as well as lawyers will be conscious of what is involved. Secondly, there is great pressure to cut delays in dealing with litigation. This comes from within the profession, from the Legal Aid Board, the Lord Chancellor's Department and the public at large. Speed of resolution being a key feature of ADR, there will be sound arguments to give the demanding client as to why a gentler approach may be called for. Thirdly, I foresee mediation, in particular, becoming part of the litigation process. Thus, it could well become common for cases to terminate after mediation and not at the court door. It will often still be vital to have forcefully conducted litigation up to the ADR session. The client will have seen his lawyer in action and will be more confident that he can hold his own.

Before I move on to the opportunities presented, there are several other problems to consider briefly. These are ethical issues that will have to be dealt with properly, to avoid the movement, and lawyers participating in it, getting a poor reputation. The first matter is the problem of unequal advice. What does the mediator do if he knows, according to his own professional standards, that a party is being permitted to enter into an agreement that is manifestly unfair or less than ought to be obtained? To some extent this has been considered earlier in the book. However, it is a major point. I addressed the litigation lawyers in the Plymouth Law Society recently, and they could foresee this as a serious problem. The worry only arises in extreme cases. When there is only doubt, but no certainty that the agreement is wrong, then the mediator cannot be sure that other, non-legal, factors are not influencing settlement and he is after all not there to decide issues. On the other hand, in the face of a blatant mistake the mediator has to decide whether or not to continue. He also has to consider his legal position, although he will normally be covered by his solicitor's Professional Indemnity Cover.

The IDR mediation agreement (Appendix 3) contains a provision entitling the mediator to withdraw at any time without giving a reason. This is to avoid showing bias by revealing his concern. However, to withdraw in this way is a radical step and could leave the mediator, or the administrative agency, open to a claim for return of fees, or worse. Short of this, he can use questioning techniques to show one party that it is moving too far. One day the situation will arise, though, where an agreement is reached in these circumstances. This could well give rise to a chorus of voices repeating the more general criticism of ADR, that it fails to achieve a just result and is much less rigorous than litigation. A partial counter to this is that 90 per cent of cases settle without the rigour of trial anyway. I feel the point is perhaps a little glib. Mediation, and other ADR processes, must be able to stand up for themselves, and not simply rely on the fact that other cases also sometimes settle unsatisfactorily. The answer to the problem, in the longer run, probably lies with correct selection of cases. In this way, and with experience, it should be possible to weed out those cases where there is an imbalance of legal ability. Alternatively, the agencies will have to give 'health warnings' to the effect that if there is any doubt about the legal (factual) implications of the case, then counsel's opinion should be sought, or the case should be taken to court.

The opportunity

Now for the more agreeable part of this chapter, the prospects for lawyers to develop their practices and learn about an enjoyable and rewarding specialism.

The first area of opportunity is to train as a third-party neutral, probably a mediator. However, until ADR is widely established and demand for neutrals is high, it is unlikely that many lawyers will get the chance to mediate regularly. Of course, it is said by some that they already often use the techniques of ADR in their practice of the law. This is true, but I am talking about organised ADR and fully-trained neutrals. In the next two or three years the case-flow will not be large enough to sustain widespread use of mediators. There is even a danger that, initially, too many people will be trained, only to discover that they get no cases. Over time the picture will improve, with supply and demand moving into balance.

If you are lucky enough to be able to practise regularly, the advantages are many. On a practical level, there is very little preparation, the work is better paid than normal judicial sittings and, importantly, the timing of the meeting is arranged to suit the convenience of everyone, including the mediator. On a professional level, the work is often challenging and satisfying. A leading QC, speaking at a conference on ADR, indicated, with a small degree of disparagement, that this type of work could never provide the buzz that comes from winning in court. Not so, is my experience. Although I have never advocated in the High Court, I know what winning a case is like and can vouch for the fact that settling a mediation can be equally invigorating. The process also provides a unique opportunity to see exactly what makes each side tick in a litigation case.

In five years I predict that there will be a professional body representing a significant number of ADR practitioners. There is already the Society of Professionals in Dispute Resolution, SPIDR, the UK chapter of an American organisation. With such a body will come a common code of conduct, standardised training and other continuing controls that distinguish a profession from, say, a trade body. Some lawyers will give up the practice of law altogether, while others will mediate most of the time, simply keeping their hand in with a bit of litigation occasionally. An interesting question is whether larger firms will open ADR departments with specialists; the City firm Masons has an ADR unit. ADR Net has started with the expectation of up to six mediators being trained in each of eighteen large regional firms of solicitors. These six will undoubtedly form the nucleus for such ADR departments. On the other hand, it is my view that there will not be a separate department because the two (ADR and litigation) are so closely connected that there would be no point in a division. A further development will be the active use of ADR in other departments. In particular, a number of lawyers I have talked to feel it has a place in the commercial field, well before anything has become at all litigious.

A second field of endeavour will be in the presentation of cases at mediation. It is here that a greater number of practitioners will have the opportunity to develop a skill and therefore a marketing tool. ADR Net and IDR have set up a parallel company known as ADR Register, consisting of professional firms interested in developing ADR in their own fields. These will be firms of lawyers and probably accountants who will be given knowledge and back-up in the theory and practice of ADR. They will be shown how to prepare and present cases in order that they can make it clear to their clients that they are in the forefront, and can provide a new service. CEDR has now expanded into the provinces and has a considerable number of professional firms as members, spread across the country. Thus, solicitors are poised to exploit ADR for the benefit of themselves and their clients.

It is interesting that, at a time when the Bar is fighting a rearguard action against solicitors in the High Court, the junior branch of the profession appears to be making all the running in ADR presentation. This could have a significant effect on the confidence of solicitors as advocates. At a mediation the solicitor will be marshalling his case and presenting it without the aid of a barrister. The case may well be large. So far, I have mediated cases as large as several hundred thousand pounds and, with costs included, the sums at stake have been considerable. In time, this will give solicitors more and more confidence, and their clients too. Admittedly, the complexities of an English trial, the rules of evidence and so on are absent, but the case nevertheless has to be handled with competence and ability.

There is at present a strong tendency for solicitors of all types to defer to Counsel, yet it is not so often that a case is so complex or so novel that it cannot be resolved without Counsel — particularly when there are good commercial reasons for an agreement. The growth of ADR could lead to greater independence from the Bar and less reliance on it where ADR is appropriate. Does this then mean that barristers are seriously threatened by the movement? Probably no more so than by the increase in the County Court jurisdiction to £50,000 (and in many cases without ceiling) and the vast increase in the number of cases that will be heard in that court. The Bar has responded by trying to curtail the expansion of rights of audience, but more importantly, it has also started to look outwards. It now actively promotes itself not only to law firms, but also to other professionals and in the UK and abroad. It has begun to look at the way barristers operate and to make improvements. Individual barristers are less willing to sit and take what comes. They are more prepared to move chambers and be pro-active than they were ten or fifteen years ago. The Bar Council has endorsed a proposal for conciliation — in the County Court! Given that a lot of barristers are able, articulate and well-connected, all this suggests to me that they can easily cope with the threat and may well draw strength from ADR. In a complex industrial democracy with surplus income, it is unlikely that traditional sources of work will dry up. Some barristers may be poised to become more closely involved in the subject. If they can suppress their egos somewhat, and make their presence inoffensive rather than assertive, they will undoubtedly make good mediators. The analysis will be easily handled and the parties should be persuaded to settle by pure charm. Of course it won't be that simple; but the process is about a lot more than assiduous, honest brokering. The pattern in the United States is for certain individuals to gain a reputation for excellence as mediators. Some barristers have a flair, intuition or charisma that will enable them to influence the parties swiftly. They should become sought-after mediators, and in time they will get the reputation for being top-quality neutrals. However, the Bar is small and before solicitor readers begin to resent the praise contained in the above sentences, the head start obtained by solicitors will probably ensure that they retain the lead in ADR developments.

It might just come about that the greatest threat to the legal profession, in the context of ADR, will arrive from outside it. By this I mean that the large firms of accountants are already showing considerable interest. One mediation referred to ADR Net was sent by a large multi-national accountancy practice. These firms are interested in litigation and a lot have litigation support units. They are financially powerful, and as their commercial clients become more aware of the subject, they may feel impelled to become closely involved. I am conscious that some solicitors see accountants as a threat in a variety of fields, including tax, probate and general litigation. However, in those cases where there is already a considerable legal element, accountants are likely to feel safer deferring to lawyers, both as mediators and as presenters. Nevertheless, in other cases where resort to the courts is not automatically seen as the next step, accountants might begin to use ADR, and ADR techniques, without lawyers. Even if this comes about, it is not a reason for lawyers to reject ADR; rather it is an argument that they must be on their mettle and be able to react swiftly. ADR Net and IDR have sufficient confidence to be inviting accountants to join the ADR Register.

I.D.R. Europe Ltd – Mediation Procedures

Unless otherwise agreed in writing by the parties, the Mediator, and I.D.R. Europe Ltd all Mediations conducted by I.D.R. Europe Ltd shall be held in accordance with these Mediation Procedures.

1. The Mediator shall not have the power or authority to tender a binding decision or an award in the dispute nor force a party to accept a settlement.

2. The parties agree to negotiate in good faith and confirm that representatives who will appear on their behalf at the Mediation Sessions will have the authority to commit and bind them to any agreement arrived at through mediation.

3. Prior to the commencement of the Mediation the parties shall enter into an Agreement to Mediate, the form and content of which shall be proposed from time to time by I.D.R. Europe Ltd.

4. Prior to the commencement of the mediation the parties shall agree upon a Mediator suggested by I.D.R. Europe Ltd.

5. No person shall serve as mediator in any dispute in which that person has any financial or personal interest. Furthermore, a Mediator agreed upon by the parties has a duty to disclose in writing to the parties prior to the commencement of the Mediation any facts or circumstances which may give rise to an appearance or presumption of bias, lack of independence, or partial interest on his part in the outcome of the Mediation or which might prevent him from proceeding diligently and effectively with the Mediation. Should either party object to the agreed Mediator within five days after such disclosure, then that Mediator shall withdraw and another shall be agreed upon. The parties recognise that the mediator is an independent contractor and not an agent or employee of I.D.R. Europe Ltd.

6. The costs of the Mediation depend upon the nature of the dispute and the amount of mediator time involved. The costs include a basic administrative fee and an hourly mediator's fee. These fees shall be paid jointly by the parties or, if agreed otherwise, in such other proportion as the parties have agreed. Prior to commencement of the Mediation the administrative and mediator fees as provided for in the Agreement to Mediate shall be paid. If a dispute is settled after all necessary parties have agreed to mediate, either orally or in writing with an Agreement to Mediate but before the first Mediation Session is held, I.D.R. Europe Ltd is entitled to only its administrative fee.

7. I.D.R. Europe Ltd will arrange with the parties and the Mediator a convenient date, time and place for the Mediation Session. Arrangements for any subsequent Mediation Session will be agreed upon by the parties and the Mediator.

8. The Mediator shall establish the order and procedures for the Mediation Session.

9. The Mediator may request the parties to provide in writing in advance of the first Mediation Session certain specified information or materials which he believes necessary to permit him to conduct the Mediation in an expeditions and orderly manner.

At the first Mediation Session the parties will be expected to produce all information reasonably required by the Mediator to understand the dispute. Should a party desire to submit additional information which is not in its possession but which it reasonably believes to be in the possession of the other party, then the parties shall negotiate in good faith on the procedures for obtaining and presenting such additional information.

10. At the mediation Session the Mediator will meet both parties together and may meet with a party separately as and when the Mediator at his sole discretion feels that private meetings ('caucuses') are appropriate.

11. Any information disclosed to the Mediator in a caucus will remain confidential and will not be disclosed by the Mediator without the prior consent of the party which conveyed such information.

12. With the written consent of the parties the Mediator may request the opinion of independent third party experts. The results of this consultation shall be reported by the Mediator to the parties and the costs thereof shall be borne by the parties.

13. Mediation Sessions are settlement negotiations and are Without Prejudice to the rights of the parties. All statements, information and material, made, given or exchanged, orally or in writing either during the Mediation Sessions or prior thereto or thereafter upon the request of the Mediator shall be inadmissible in any legal proceedings, in court or arbitration, to the maximum extent permitted by law. Evidence which is otherwise admissible shall not be rendered inadmissible as a result of its use in the Mediation Sessions. The parties agree not to summon or otherwise require the Mediator or any representative of I.D.R. Europe Ltd to appear or testify or produce records, notes, or any other information or material in any legal proceedings, in court or arbitration, and no recordings or stenographic records will be made of the Mediation Sessions.

14. Any agreement reached by the parties through the Mediation shall be set down in writing and duly executed by their authorised representatives.

15. The parties may be represented by a legal adviser at any stage of the mediation process and are encouraged to take legal advice as and when they feel it is necessary. Should a party choose to have a legal adviser present at the Mediation Sessions it shall so advise I.D.R. Europe Ltd at least seven days before the mediation Session. The parties recognise that neither the Mediator nor I.D.R. Europe Ltd will be acting as a legal adviser or legal representative for either of the parties in the mediation. The Mediator and I.D.R. Europe Ltd have no duty to assert, analyse or protect any legal right or obligation of either of the parties including encumbrance rights, statute of limitations, or any other claim requirement, and they are under no duty to make any independent analysis of the dispute nor to raise issues not raised by the parties themselves nor to determine that additional parties should participate in the Mediation.

16. The Mediation shall be termianted either by the execution of an agreement by the parties resolving their dispute or by a declaration by either party, or the Mediator, that the Mediation shall be then terminated.

ADR Net Ltd – Mediator Agreement

This agreement is made this _____ day of _____ 19   between:

I.D.R. Europe Ltd., (the 'Company'), and _____ (the 'Mediator')

WHEREAS:

(i)   The Mediator is a Solicitor and a partner or employee of a firm of Solicitors belonging to ADR Net Ltd ('ADR Net'),

(ii)   The Mediator has completed the Mediator Traning Course conducted by the Company and has expressed his/her interest in accepting referrals from the Company to act as a mediator in mediations arranged by the Company, and

(iii) The Company has offered to include the Mediator in its panel of mediators and from time to time to propose to parties in dispute his/her appointment to mediate their dispute in accordance with the appointment rotation procedures agreed with ADR Net.

NOW THEREFORE IT HAS BEEN AGREED:

1. Inclusion in panel

The Company hereby agrees to include the Mediator in its panel of mediators and from time to time to propose the Mediator for the mediation of disputes which are in the sole opinion of the Company compatible with the Mediator's professional expertise and mediation experience.

2. Acceptance of mediations

The Mediator may decline his/her appointment as mediator of a particular dispute without cause. Should the Mediator accept such an appointment then he/she shall perform the role and duties of mediator in accordance with the terms and conditions of this agreement, the Company's Code of Conduct for Mediators, the Agreement to Mediate, the Rules of Membership of ADR Net, and all other applicable procedures set by the Company and ADR Net, and advised to the Mediator.

3. Mediator's fees and expenses

3.1 The Mediator's fee for all mediations accepted shall be calculated and paid for on an hourly basis with a minimum of five hours at the applicable rate plus VAT. Preparation time and follow up shall be charged in addition only with the agreement of the Company on a case by case basis.

3.2 The Mediator shall be entitled to be paid fees for travelling time and for related expenses reasonably incurred. Such payment shall be at the current rate set by the Company and ADR Net from time to time.

3.3 The Company will collect from the parties, with the assistance of the Mediator if so requested, the Mediator's fees and expenses. After each mediation session, the Mediator shall ensure that the parties complete and sign a timesheet indicating the length of the Mediation Session, and the Mediator shall then promptly submit to the Company a Time and Expense Statement, in a form provided by the Company, detailing his/her time and expenses for that particular mediation. Within fourteen days of receipt of the relevant Time and Expense Statement the Company shall remit to the mediator the funds due thereunder.

3.4 Notwithstanding that the Company shall be responsible for paying the Mediator's fees and expenses, the Mediator shall use his/her reasonable endeavours to ensure that the said fees and expenses are collected from the parties, for example:

3.4.1 in the event of the mediation session overrunning the pre-paid period
— through obtaining signatures on the above mentioned timesheet, and/or
3.4.2 there being further mediation session(s) on separate day(s)
— through advising the Company that such session(s) will be held, at least seven days prior thereto, so as to enable the Company to obtain pre-payment of the expected fees and expenses prior to the mediation session(s) being held.

3.5 The Company shall be entitled to retain 10% of the Mediator's hourly fees as an administrative charge.

4. Errors and omissions insurance

Unless the Mediator is otherwise covered in the performance of his/her services hereunder through his/her existing solicitors' professional indemnity insurance with the Solicitors Indemnity Fund or other insurer, the Company shall upon being requested by the Mediator include and maintain the Mediator within the coverage of its current Errors and Omissions Insurance, at no cost to the Mediator, and provide the Mediator with a copy of the policy upon request.

5. Independent contractor

The Mediator is an independent contractor and shall not represent himself/herself to be an employee, agent or representative of the Company.

6. Confidentiality and restrictive covenant

6.1 The Mediator recognises and acknowledges that mediation is a relatively new field in the resolution of commercial disputes and there is little public information and data available on the training of mediators and actual mediation procedures and techniques. The Mediator also recognises and acknowledges that the Company and ADR Net are relative leaders in the field and the information and data which the Mediator will learn through his/her association with the Company and ADR Net, is of significant value and the Company and ADR Net have legitimate and substantial interests in having such information and data remain confidential and a trade secret to the extent permitted by law.

6.2 In view of the foregoing and in consideration for the Company having provided mediator training to the Mediator and agreeing to enter into this agreement the Mediator agrees:

6.2.1 throughout the period of this agreement and for a period of one year thereafter:

– the Mediator shall not be involved with as an investor, principal, director, employee or consultant, including acting as a mediator, any organization offering and/or administering mediation programmes in the UK for the resolution of commercial disputes other than the Company and ADR Net, and
– the Mediator shall not act as a mediator in disputes involving parties with whom the Mediator has previously acted in mediations arranged by the Company without the participation therein of the Company as the administrator.
– Notwithstanding the foregoing throughout the aforesaid period and thereafter the Mediator shall be free to act as a mediator in mediations arranged solely by the Mediator on his or her own initiative.

6.2.2 to retain at all times as private and confidential such information, data, and business secrets concerning the affairs of the Company, ADR Net and the parties to the respective mediations as the Mediator shall gain as a result of receiving mediator training, acting as a mediator pursuant hereto, or participation in or with ADR Net.

6.3 In the event of the lawful termination of the Marketing and Administrative Agreement of the 21st December 1990 between the Company and ADR Net within the period provided for in 6.2.1 above, then as of the date of termination of the aforesaid Agreement the period provided for in 6.2.1 shall concurrently end.

7. Termination

This agreement may be terminated by either party at any time on seven days advance written notice, provided however that after tendering such notice, if so requested by the Company, the Mediator shall complete according to the terms and conditions of this Agreement all mediations for which he/she has been selected as a mediator by the parties prior to the date of such notice.

8. Dispute resolution

8.1 Any dispute or differences between the parties hereto arising out of or in any way connected with this agreement shall first be referred to mediation in accordance with the then applicable mediation procedures of the Company. The Mediator shall be agreed upon by the parties and failing such agreement within 15 days of one party suggesting the appointment of a mediator and providing their suggestion therefor, the Mediator shall be appointed by the then presiding President of the Law Society.

8.2 Should the parties fail to reach agreement on their dispute or difference through the aforesaid mediation, then the dispute or difference shall be finally resolved by arbitration by a sole arbitrator to be appointed in the absence of agreement between the parties by the aforesaid President and conducted according to English law.

IN WITNESS WHEREOF the parties have set their hands as of the day and year first above written.

I.D.R. EUROPE LTD   THE MEDIATOR

_____   _____

By:

I.D.R. Europe Ltd – Agreement to mediate

NAMES: _____

hereby agree to have I.D.R. Europe Ltd, administer the mediation of their dispute concerning:

_____

on the following terms and conditions:

1. Mediation procedures

The Mediation shall be held and conducted according to this Agreement to Mediate and the current Mediation Procedures of I.D.R. Europe Ltd, attached hereto and incorporated herein.

2. Mediator

The parties agree that _____ will be the Mediator. The parties recognise that the Mediator is an independent contractor and not an agent or employee of I.D.R. Europe Ltd.

3. Mediation fees

(a) The Mediator's fees will be charged at the rate of £ _____ per hour with a minimum charge of five hours plus an administrative fee of £ _____ , both plus VAT. The parties agree to prepay Mediation Fees as follows:

Amount _____

Payable by _____

Amount _____

Payable by _____

and the parties understand that the Mediation Session will not take place until such fees are prepaid as provided for.

(b) At the end of each Mediation Session the parties and the Mediator shall prepare and sign a timesheet indicating the length of that Session.

(c) Any charges for Mediation Fees in excess of the amount on deposit shall be paid within seven days in equal proportions or, if agreed otherwise, in such other proportions as the parties have agreed. Expenses and travel time shall be paid to the Mediator in accordance with I.D.R. Europe Ltd. policy. At the conclusion of the mediation, after deduction of the administrative fee, the fee for the Mediator's time and the reimbursement of expenses, any unused pre-paid Mediation Fees will be promptly returned to the parties in the proportions in which they were pre-paid.

4. Consulting with legal advisers

Any party not represented by a legal adviser or in appropriate cases other professional adviser is advised to consult one before, during and after the Mediation Session and before finalising an agreement reached pursuant to the Mediation. The parties recognise that neither I.D.R. Europe Ltd, nor the Mediator is giving legal advice or acting as a lawyer for any of the parties or analysing or protecting any party's legal rights.

5. Private Sessions

The Mediator may hold private sessions with only one party. These private sessions are designed to improve the Mediator's understanding of the party's position. Information gained by the Mediator through such a session is confidential unless (a) it is in any event publicly available or (b) the Mediator is specifically authorised to disclose it.

6. Confidentiality

(a) The parties recognise that the Mediation Sessions are for the purpose of attempting to achieve a negotiated settlement and as such are without prejudice and will be inadmissible in any litigation or arbitration of the dispute. Evidence which is otherwise admissible shall not be rendered inadmissible as a result of its use in the Mediation Session. The parties will not subpoena or otherwise require I.D.R. Europe Ltd. or the Mediator or any other person attending the mediation under the auspices of I.D.R. Europe Ltd. to testify or produce records, notes or any other information or material whatsoever in any future or continuing proceedings.

(b) All documents, statements, information and other material produced or given for or during the Mediation, whether in writing or orally, shall be held in confidence by the parties and shall be used solely for the purposes of the Mediation. At the termination of the Mediation all such material shall be returned to the originating party or forthwith destroyed at their option.

7. Termination of mediation session

Either of the parties or the mediator shall be entitled in their absolute discretion to terminate a Mediation Session at any time without giving any reason therefor.

Name: _____   Name: _____

Address: _____   Address: _____

_____   _____

_____   _____

_____   _____

Date: _____   Date: _____

Signed: _____   Signed: _____

Accepted to administer the mediation as provided for:

Date: _____

Signed: _____

     I.D.R. Europe Ltd

Case Studies

I. PERSONAL INJURY MEDIATION JULY 1991

1. Facts

1.1 Motorcycle accident. Plaintiff pillion passenger on former husband's bike, he rode into a roundabout and she broke both lower legs and suffered surgical and psychogenic shock.

1.2 The couple initially claimed there was another vehicle which had contributed to the accident. Both later retracted this assertion, thus showing that they both lacked some credibility as witnesses.

1.3 The former husband was the Defendant, represented by his insurers. He had been arrested for drunk driving and had already had two previous disqualifications for like offences. However, there was a mix-up with samples and he was acquitted. At the time of the prosecution, he told the police that his drinks had been laced. Although he could now admit drinking (the figure was twice the limit) as he couldn't be prosecuted again, this would make his evidence look doubtful.

1.4 The Plaintiff, who was 21 at the time of the accident, had been a clerk for a freight company and had had a solid work record in this field since leaving school. After the accident she was off work for 19 months and then set up her own business. This failed after 8 months and apart from a month working as a clerk, with mobility difficulties, she had been unemployed since. A serious problem became clear. The last medical report was 2 years old and then the doctor had said that the Plaintiff could go back to work in 6 months. She was now saying that the pain and swelling of her legs meant she could not work and might not be able to for a long time. This had a bearing on both general damages and future losses.

2. Legal issues

2.1 The issue of contributory negligence arose on the basis that if the Defendant could prove the Plaintiff KNEW he was riding whilst under the influence of excessive alcohol, then up to 25% 'con neg' would be awarded. On the one hand the reading had been twice the legal norm and the Defendant had a pattern of drinking and driving. Furthermore, the Plaintiff's credibility had been tainted by the reference to a fictitious motorist. On the other hand, the Defendant had maintained that his drinks were laced and he didn't know he was over the limit. Additionally, case law provided instances of experts confirming that even twice over the limit, a largish man would not necessarily show symptoms of drunkennes.

2.2 The only real legal issue on the measure of damages arose over whether a judge would award future loss damages on the basis of a partial loss with a multiplier (high because she was young, but reduced by virtue of marriage prospects) or whether he would allow a Smith and Manchester element only.

3. Mediation

3.1 Present were the Plaintiff, her solicitor and her barrister; together with the insurer's claims manager, the insurer's solicitor and a junior claims handler.

3.2 The session got off to bad start with the defence party arriving 25 minutes late and immediately complaining about the smoke in the room.

3.3 The Defendant's solicitor was a powerful and effective lawyer but needed to be:

(a) handled with care, since she was hostile to the process, but

(b) kept fully occupied and stimulated, since there was the risk that she would take literally the concept of voluntariness – and walk out.

The strategies I adopted were to be as nice as possible (without crawling) and to allow her face-to-face contact with the barrister on the other side, to enable her to gather a lot of data and argument from him, in the hope that this would give her sufficient material to work on during the private sessions. As to being nice, this was not difficult. I gathered that she felt a few corns had been trodden on in the build-up to the agreement to mediate: I talked through these issues and made soothing noises. I told her frankly that she was probably the most competent lawyer I had dealt with (which was true) but also very precise which presented me with a challenge in this ADR forum. We also discovered that we had both, in the past, prosecuted for the police. Whenever she was getting too tough, I jokingly said 'I'm very glad I didn't come up against you in court' – this was no lie.

3.4 The Plaintiff's barrister was a different personality altogether. He was the first barrister I had dealt with in a mediation. He was intelligent and articulate, handling the arguments with ease. He was not being particularly tough. Perhaps the biggest problem he posed was that, in common with his branch of the profession, he was aloof. He had not lived with the case for long periods and did not know the Plaintiff well. Accordingly, it was not a matter of personal importance to him if the case settled, so long as he had operated within his professional guidelines. My strategy with him, as this was a legal aid case, was to stress his obligations to the Fund, to make the most of his weak points, but not to seek to develop any personal rapport, other than to endeavour to earn his respect. I felt the relationship between he two branches of the legal profession suggested this to be the right approach. It was pointed out to me that he was not a PI specialist. I avoided rubbing this point in.

3.5 Fairly soon into the mediation it became clear that to settle the case would require both sides taking a risk on what an updated medical report would reveal: either the Plaintiff was a lot worse, in which case the Defence would have to revise upwards, or she wasn't, in which case the Plaintiff was lacking in credibility even more, and stood the risk of getting even less than on offer at the mediation. In these circumstances, with competent lawyers, and in the light of my strategy for dealing with the Defence lawyer, I called an early meeting with the two lawyers alone. We soon established that on a maximum view the Plaintiff was asking for £171,000 and the Defence valued the case at £16,000. Even after the barrister offered to 'share the risk' I felt it would be necessary to abort early.

3.6 However, it was a good idea to get all the cards on the table early on. The Defence went away to study their risks; the barrister was concerned about the size of his own figure. Initially, the huge difference had been in the assessment of future losses/Smith and Manchester. However, once the 'global figure' negotiations started, the real issue emerged. This was the valuation of general damages. The Defence offered £18,500 as an opening shot. The Plaintiff came down to £55,000. The day ended with the parties respectively at £25,000 and £38,000. No further movement could be achieved, particularly as the Defence lawyer had announced that she must leave by 4.30 (a situation to be avoided at all costs if possible). During the later stages of bargaining, future losses were reduced dramatically but the Plaintiff still felt her pain, suffering and loss of amenity were being undervalued. On advice, she decided to take the risk of an adverse medical report.

4. Conclusions

This case would undoubtedly have settled if a current doctor's report had been available. Even so there was a chance of settlement. The barrister had effectively conceded that he must negotiate on the present report but sadly, there was insufficient consensus on the implications of this. Interestingly, the barrister had opened by saying that his client was going to use the money to buy a house. This was the 'interest-based bargaining' beloved of ADR purists. There was the opportunity for the mediator to invite her to be reasonable in order to take advantage of a buyer's house market. There was also a downside. The Defence lawyer was apprehensive that a claim worth a house was 'going through the roof'. To change the metaphor, the initial claim was 'telephone numbers' compared to her evaluation of the damages; the Plaintiff's credibility had suffered. Despite all this, the day was not wasted. Issues were clarified and narrowed, risks were considered. Settlement should have been brought forward radically.

II. PERSONAL INJURY MEDIATION AUGUST 1991

1. Introduction

I did a mediation recently with Derek Bellew as an ADR Net observer training to be a mediator himself. He very kindly did me a report which is set out below. The purpose of including this report is to show the mediation session from the viewpoint of a third party. It can be seen that there are criticisms and it was unfortunate that on this occasion the plaintiff was not present – *A.B.*

Abbreviations
'D' – defendant
'I's R' – insurer's representatives (Claims Manager and solicitor)
'P' – plaintiff
'P's S' – plaintiff's solicitor
'Mediator' – Alex Bevan

2. Facts

P was injured in an accident admittedly caused by the negligence of D, the driver of a Porsche car. P suffered severe fracture to her leg, and was likely to suffer some long-term discomfort etc. P's husband (a car worker) was also injured in the accident, but his claim had been settled. P had been employed as a hairdresser, but had then taken over a café. She and her husband lived in a flat above the café. Prior to the accident, the café had produced a profit, net, of £847 per month.

After the accident she kept the business going between April 1987 and September 1988. During that period she had to take on additional staff, which affected the profitability of the business. She had various operations on her leg, and she found it increasingly difficult to cope with the work in the café — during the evenings, in particular, her leg swelled up, and she suffered discomfort. In September 1988, accordingly, she sold the café for a total of £130,000, and she and her husband purchased a house for £98,000. She had not worked since September 1988. The medical report stated that she would not be able to do any work, for the foreseeable future, involving prolonged standing or movement. She would, however, it was thought, be able to do 'mainly sedentary' work. P is now aged 49, and has relatively few (if any) academic, or other formal, qualifications.

3. Preliminaries

Prior to the start of proceedings, it transpired, to the surprise of I's R, that P was not herself attending the mediation, but was to be represented solely by her solicitor. I's R indicated that this was not satisfactory, as they wanted an opportunity personally to see her and assess the credibility of her claims. P's S indicated that they had instructions and would negotiate in good faith but any settlement would be subject to final confirmation from P. It was agreed that the mediation would proceed on this basis.

4. Mediator's introduction

The Mediator indicated that the aim was to come to a settlement, but he accepted that it would be a non-binding agreement only because of P's absence.

The process was intended to be entirely flexible.

He would ask the parties to state their figures first in their opening statements, and that there would be no negotiation during that process.

All proceedings were without prejudice, and confidential.

Nothing said in the mediation would be disclosed to the outside world in general, nor would statements by one party made to the Mediator, in private session, be disclosed to the other party, without the authority of the person making them.

The process was entirely voluntary, and either side was free to leave at any time.

The process was non-binding, and there was no power on the Mediator to determine the outcome.

The Mediator would act as a Chairman, clarifying issues and leading the discussion. He would aim to act as a 'devil's advocate', and ask tough questions.

He stressed that it was not his job to form any opinion as to the respective merits of the case.

5. P's S's opening

P's claim was put forward. It consisted of the following elements:

Items 1–4 – Damage to clothing, personal effects, medical treatment, increased wages incurred between April 1987 and July 1987, and increased wages July 1988 – September 1988. These totalled about £4,000.

Item 5 – loss of income from the business, September 1988 – September 1991. This was claimed at three years' loss × £847 net per month = £30,500.

Item 6 – Interest on the above.

Item 7 – Future loss, taking a multiple of 5, and multiplicand (£847 × 12 months) of £10,000 = claim of £50,000.

Item 8 – General damages – £20,000 to £25,000.

Item 9 – Interest on general damages.

6. I's R's response

The problem was the 'specials' claimed in the total sum of £85,000 excluding general damages. This was the 'loss' arising out of the sale of the business. The insurers were anxious that the accident was not being taken advantage of as an 'excuse' to 'get out of the business' — 'to retire early'. The insurers would need to be convinced that P had had to get out of the business. Should she not have managed with part-time additional staff?

They might need an accountant's advice before any trial.

They would have liked to have asked P in person about whether she had actively tried to obtain 'sedentary work'. P's S responded, quoting from an attendance note made on her, that P had difficulty staying on her feet, and had no typing/secretarial skills. She could not return to work. It was not possible for her to re-train.

I's R said they might need an assessment from an independent employment consultant, but they were very sceptical that she would be 'unemployable' for the next twelve years.

7. Private sessions

The proceedings then went into private sessions. There were four such sessions with P's S, and three sessions with I's R.

1st Session with P's S
P's S produced an extract of Counsel's advice dealing with the claim for 'general' damage.

Reference was made to the settlement of P's husband's claim.

Some of the questions put to P's S were:

(1) Would P have continued in the café until she was 60?

(2) Was there any element of betterment in the fact that the house they now lived in was clearly far preferable to the flat above the café? (P still retained the mortgage of £41,000 which previously had been offset against the profits of the café.) Could they not have obtained part-time staff? (The cost of part-time staff, of the right kind, and to cover the necessary hours, would have amounted to the £10,000 claimed by way of loss of profits.)

(3) Was it reasonable mitigation to sell the business?

(4) Could she reasonably have continued to work with part-time staff in the café?

(5) Could she reasonably find other alternative work?

1st Session with I's R
With the I's R, discussion took place on the general damages. Recent photographs were examined of the condition of P, which had been supplied by P's S, but I's R stressed that they would have liked to have seen her in person. They thought the claim for general damages was a little high.

Their main contest was on the specials. They felt she could be doing something. She was clearly an enterprising lady if she had been able to take over and run a café. Most of all, however, they thought she should have 'soldiered on'.

She carried on for some fifteen months after the accident. Why had she given up in September 1988? She could have continued to employ temporary staff (the cost of which was provisionally put at £6,000). There were no 'psychological symptoms' making it impossible for her to continue work. They thought that temporary staff could have been obtained at £2 per hour.

The first session with I's R finished with an agreement on their part that they would produce figures to respond to the opening claim by P's S.

2nd session with P's S
The Mediator then returned to P's S. The latter felt that P had 'soldiered on', had spent extra money on staff, but it was just not possible to make the profit which would have justified continuing the business.

There was clear medical evidence of the swelling in her legs at the end of the day. She had lost 'motivation and drive'. He was not satisfied that she could have continued to work in the café.

He then did concede that he recognised that he might be at risk, on certain issues, before a judge. He recognised that this did mean that he might have to offer a discount on her full claim for damages to take account of the risk factor here.

He thought that £2 per hour was much too low for the realistic cost of additional staff.

2nd session with I's R
Private session, then returned to I's R.

They conceded items 1–4 for the purposes of the mediation, but felt that they were otherwise open to attack.

Their main contest, however, was on the future losses, and on those incurred up to September 1991. She should have used part-time staff. Accordingly on item 5 they would substitute £12,000 instead of the £30,000 asked for.

Item 6 was no problem.

On item 7 they thought the multiplier ought to be 4 (not 5). The multiplicand would be £4,000, making a total offer under (7) of £16,000.

On item 8 they would offer £17,500.

Item 9 was agreed in principle.

They assessed the time of the trial at being 1½–2 days and recognised the need for specialist witnesses etc.

3rd session with P's S
Private session then resumed with P's S.

He was prepared to offer a discount on loss up to September 1991. He would reduce this figure by one third down to £20,000. Even if there was, however, merit in the I's R argument that P should have found alternative employment, there would have had to have been a period of training etc. He would similarly reduce a claim for future loss by about one third, bringing the claim down to £35,000.

He wanted £22,500 for 'general' damages.

He assessed P's claim as being worth a minimum of £87,500 – £90,000, and the Mediator was authorised to put this figure back to I's R.

3rd session with I's R
In resumed discussions with I's R, it was first of all acknowledged that there was an error in the previous calculation, but as the figure related to interest only it did not seem to matter (the Mediator had put the offer to P's S as being worth £60,000 – it was worth this if interest had been added on to the opening offer put forward by I's R).

I's R made an important concession. They had accepted the strength of P's S's argument that there would have been a training period even if (as they thought) she should have found alternative employment. They were, therefore, prepared to accept the loss to September 1991 at £20,000.

They were prepared to increase their offer on 'general' damages to £20,000 (representing the 'minimum' figure of P). They were prepared to increase the multiplicand for future loss to £5,000, but would retain the 'multiplier' at 4.

This offer was now worth £60,000 plus interest, which could take it above £70,000.

4th session with P's S
The final private session then took place with P's S. Unfortunately, P's S felt that he could not reduce his claim below £87,500. It appeared that he had advised P that the 'minimum' settlement range was this figure. He could not go below it.

The Mediator was clearly in a difficulty. He did not want the insurers to be put in a position where they were constantly being expected to 'increase' their offer, without response from P. To achieve a settlement it is possible that the insurers would have gone higher, but they clearly could not be expected to do so in the absence of any concession from P.

8. Final open session

The Mediator thanked the parties for participating and summarised the proceedings as follows:

8.1 The insurers might go above £72,000, 'but not today'.

8.2 He regretted the absence of P, but relied on P's S to report fully to her on what had transpired.

8.3 He thought it was important that 'dialogue' should be kept open between the parties, and the insurers said they would welcome the opportunity to do this.

8.4 The possibility was foreseen of the insurer's meeting with P and reviewing their position in the light of that meeting.

9. Concluding remarks

P's S repeated that there could have been 'no advantage' if his client had been present. He was prepared to continue further dialogue.

I's R confirmed that they were prepared to continue dialogue, but wished that P had been present to have heard the process. It was stressed, finally, that the 'concession' made by the insurers in respect of Items 1–5 was for the purposes of the mediation only, and they reserved the right fully to challenge the claims under this head, and it could not be assumed that the other proposals would remain open.

10. Conclusions and comment of the Observer

10.1 It was frankly uncanny as to the extent in which the situations envisaged by 'role-play' in training sessions had been replicated in the real-life situation.

10.2 I feel that it is extremely important that the Mediator should deal with both sides in exactly the same way. I think it was unfortunate that the Mediator had previously mediated a case involving the insurer's representative and, from the start, referred to the Claims Manager by his Christian name (although the insurer's solicitor was referred to as 'Mr'), whereas the Plaintiff's solicitor was throughout referred to as 'Mr'. This did not affect, in any way, the way the day's proceedings went, but if the Plaintiff had been there, I think there would have been a danger that she would have thought that there was some kind of 'cosy' relationship between IDR and the insurers. She would, perhaps, have felt that she was being 'soft-touched' into a settlement unfavourable to her.

10.3 It was unsatisfactory that the Plaintiff was not present. It is most important that 'ordinary' citizens actually do *see* the process at work, to understand how under less formal cross-examination etc the strengths and weaknesses of both their own case, and that of the opposition, can materially affect the outcome. I feel confident that if the Plaintiff had been personally present, then there would have been a number of possible consequences:

   (i)   the insurance company could have assessed whether she was a 'malingerer' or a person genuinely trying to cope with her disability;
   (ii) she could have clarified questions of fact, where these were in doubt;
   (iii) she could well have arrived at the view that some reduction on the £87,500 was in her interests and that a slightly lower settlement would have been arrived at with which she would have been perfectly happy.

10.4 Apart from the above observations, however, it can unquestionably be said that the mediation was a success even though no agreement was reached. The Mediator handled the proceedings with great skill and in particular challenged a number of 'assumptions' which produced very useful concessions from both sides, which eased the way towards a settlement.

It is very interesting that the Plaintiffs started off with a band of settlement between £87,500 and £120,000, whereas the Defendants started with a band of £50,000 – £70,000 (but without interest). With the capacity for movement which the Plaintiff's presence might have had it seems likely that the process of mediation would have produced a result which was higher than the insurers would have liked, lower than the Plaintiff had been advised, but was nevertheless, by any assessment, a 'fair' result to both sides.

10.5 It was extremely interesting how the mediation process enabled negotiation to go on what were essentially 'parallel' lines. The Plaintiff was saying that she acted reasonably in giving up the café, but recognised that there was a risk that it could be held that she should have tried harder to find alternative work. The Defendants, on the other hand, still felt strongly that she should have continued the café, and that they would argue the case on that basis. Interestingly enough, the extra costs of running the café (in the form of part-time workers etc) were not too dissimilar from the kind of 'mitigation' figures which the Plaintiff's representatives were inclined to concede.

10.6 It was extremely interesting how quickly, in practice, both sides were able, in the course of private session, actually to move from stated 'positions' to recognition of 'interest' which applied to their own case, and that of the other side.

10.7 Some scepticism has been expressed as to whether mediation is a suitable process for personal injury claims like this, which ought to be capable of settlement by means of direct negotiation between competent solicitors. This Observer's judgement (and he stresses that he is not a practitioner in this field at all) is that the mediation process, during the course of a period of three to four hours, made much faster strides toward settlement than could ever take place by means of 'without prejudice' correspondence, or direct debate.

The reason for this is quite clear. Both parties to the proceedings felt far more able to make concessions as to the weaknesses of their own cases in private session to the mediator than they would ever feel free to do in any kind of formal process.

It is also extremely significant that where such concessions were made then both sides were prepared, after due reflection, to authorise the fact of those concessions to be communicated to the other side — this was particularly so when it was clear that both sides were making concessions, because they wanted to reach a settlement.

These notes are being dictated two days after the event, but this Observer feels confident that, as a result of the mediation, settlement will be effected before trial, that the mediation will have contributed materially towards that settlement, and that the settlement will unquestionaly be founded on a fairer and more realistic assessment of the issues than would otherwise have been the case.

APPENDIX 5

Case Histories

I. COMPUTER MEDIATION OCTOBER 1988

This case history shows how the flexibility of mediation can be used as different circumstances require it. The normal model consists of a joint session followed by private meetings, but this case was settled by having a private meeting first, followed by a joint session, followed by one further private meeting.

The case involved a small business which had purchased a computer system and then commissioned a software company to write a program to computerise its manual system for stock control. The program was duly written and installed; unfortunately it did not work properly. Two or three visits were made by the software company to put things right but to no avail. At this point the businessman refused to pay the outstanding balance of the software company's bill, and the software company refused to do any more work until the bill had been paid. A typical 'Mexican standoff'.

The businessman, having heard about mediation, contacted I.D.R. Europe who appointed as mediator a micro-computer specialist, who had been trained as a mediator. The businessman also supplied, in advance, a most comprehensive brief of the problems to date. At the subsequent private meeting it transpired that all the company really wanted was a working program, as the computer was sitting idle. The mediator then contacted the other party, explained the problem and how mediation may help. He then had a private meeting with the software company. At this point a number of issues had emerged, not least the realisation by the software company that copyright in the program was vested in the businessman, and as he intended to market the program as part of a franchise package, they would not be getting any royalities.

The mediator then proposed a joint meeting with the parties; as most of the animosity had now been defused by the mediator, this was agreed to. At this meeting several further issues were raised by both parties. At the subsequent private meetings these issues were discussed and several propositions were made. Substantial agreement had been achieved, so both parties returned to a joint session. The final agreement consisted of a withdrawal of claims and counter-claims, the drawing up of a firm specification for the final software program, and a royalty based on the rights of an author of a program. Both parties are now working together in a spirit of co-operation and trust to finish the original project.

Mediator comment: I am convinced that mediation offers a viable – perhaps in many cases the best – means of resolving complex disputes. The parties are the best judges of a fair outcome, and mediation offers them a means of exercising that judgement expeditiously, economically and in a way which enables them to preserve, rather than destroy, their relationships.

II. CONSTRUCTION MEDIATIONS OCTOBER 1988

(1) This case involved a church building which was built in 1969. It had a shallow domed roof over a central sanctuary, with building wings on either side having flat

roofs. The dome was covered with a metal roofing material, and the flat roofs were topped with standard built-up roofing. Shortly after the building was completed the dome developed leaks. Several years later, the flat roofs also began to leak. There was also a problem with the foundation drainage system, which was the apparent cause of a wet basement. During the next several years, numerous attempts were made to correct the problems, with only limited success.

In 1981 the owner issued proceedings against the architect and general contractor, who brought in the roofing sub-contractor, plumbing sub-contractor and metal roofing supplier. During the proceedings a new, higher dome was constructed over the original one. The owner sought to recover the cost of the new dome (in addition to its other damages) on the theory that the original dome was defectively designed.

I.D.R. was brought in to mediate the settlement discussions. After five hours of mediated negotiations, the case settled, with all five defendants contributing in varying amounts to the settlement 'pot'. (The owner did not recover the cost of the new dome, but an amount was paid by the architect for design problems relating to the original dome).

(2) This case involved the construction in 1978–9 of a huge distribution warehouse with a built-up insulated roof over steel decking. The roof area covered a total of 26 acres. Soon after construction was completed, serious problems began to develop in the roof membrane – splits, ridging, pulled flashing, disbonding – with resultant leaks and damage to the interior of the building and its contents.

The owner hired experts to diagnose the problem and recommend corrective action. At first it was believed that the problems were caused primarily by faulty installation of the roof membrane. Later it appeared that the faulty design and installation of the steel framing and expansion joints also might have contributed significantly to the problem.

The owner filed suit for $6 million in 1983 against the architect, general contractor, inspection company, several sub-contractors and material suppliers, on breach of contract, negligence and strict liability grounds. Other parties were brought in by way of third-party complaint. A total of ten defendants were ultimately involved – each pointing to one or more of the others as the primary cause of the plaintiff's problems.

During the ensuing years, substantial discovery was undertaken, involving the expenditure of hundreds of thousands of dollars by the parties for attorney's fees, experts and other expenses. Two settlement conferences were conducted by the court during this period, without success.

By now a total of 45 depositions had already been taken, with at least 25 more scheduled. A firm trial date was set for October 1989. Complicating the matter further was the fact that the building had been sold in December 1987 (with a discount in price for the faulty roof), leaving the owner only with its cause of action.

At the suggestion of the insurer of one of the defendants, USA&M were asked to explore with all of the parties the possibility of resolving the matter through mediation. They met twice with the attorneys and worked out a written agreement to mediate, spelling out the ground rules and the terms of engagement. Prior to the mediation the parties submitted confidential, written briefs to familiarise the mediator with their respective views of the case. A personal inspection of the roof was also made.

For three consecutive days, the mediation was conducted in the offices of a law firm. In addition to its attorney(s) each of the parties was represented at the mediation session by an executive (and/or insurance representative) who was authorised to conclude a settlement on behalf of that party. USA&M negotiated the total damage issue first and then dealt with the liability of the individual defendants. At the end of the third full day of mediation, the case settled, with all of the defendants agreeing to contribute in varying amounts to the total settlement (a seven figure amount).

III. COMMUNITY MEDIATION APRIL 1989

This case involved 6 people.

Five young women whose ages ranged from 37 to 23 had signed a 1-year lease on a house, in the sum of 300 dollars each. Two of the girls, the eldest, who had also lived in the house for 7 years already, and one other, had a lesbian relationship and had started to share a room. The defendant, the youngest girl, who had a boyfriend, and a very bubbly personality became the subject of animosity by the two lesbians who felt she was quote 'not a good house partner'.

All girls signing the lease were interviewed by the eldest before being allowed to live there but sexual proclivities were not discussed. It was a rule however that they would all be non-smokers.

After 5 months the situation became so unbearable that the youngest girl Kim decided to leave. She advertised in the local paper for a replacement who was duly interviewed and accepted. Kim then moved out. On the same day, the girl who had previously accepted her room then backed out. Subsequently the other 4 girls sued Kim for the remaining 6 months of the lease, a sum of 1800 dollars.

Kim did not have the money, and two of the other girls could not afford to increase their contribution in order to pay the 1500 dollars per month to the main landlord.

At the start of the mediation the 4 girls as joint plaintiffs complained about the presence of Tom, Kim's boyfriend. Kim maintained he was only there to give moral support. The mediator suggested that Tom took no part in the joint session, but was merely an observer. This was eventually agreed.

Both sides then stated their side of the case. The plaintiffs' evidence that the defendant was not a good house partner was limited to one bounced cheque, which subsequently cleared, and rather nebulous feelings which were not shared by all the girls – one was still friendly with Kim.

Kim accepted all the plaintiffs said, and stated that she had no wish to leave the house, in fact she could only just afford the additional 20 dollars per month that her new room was costing her.

1st Plaintiff Caucus
The plaintiffs now claimed they simply couldn't trust Kim because of the bounced cheque. They accepted that Kim could not pay anyway and suggested they would have her declared bankrupt and her car sold to pay the debt.

The mediator asked them to consider the following: Kim at present owed them nothing – the rent was for the next 6 months. Would a Judge be likely to rule on a future debt?

In trying to replace Kim, were they setting their standards too high?

Why had they not anticipated this problem at the interview?

1st defence caucus
Kim really could not understand why she was being sued, she liked all the girls, and felt very aggrieved at being pushed out especially as her new room was costing more. As a goodwill gesture she was prepared to pay 150 dollars if they would drop the case. She stated that it was the eldest girl who really ran the house as she had lived there for so long.

2nd plaintiff caucus
The mediator relayed the offer of 150 dollars to the plaintiffs.

The plaintiffs then put forward the proposal that Kim should only pay if they could not find a replacement, up to a maximum of 900 dollars, i.e. 3 months. The mediator stated he would relay this to Kim, but in the meantime would they think about what would happen if Kim counterclaimed against them firstly for harassment secondly because she was now having to pay more for her new room.

2nd defence caucus
The new offer was talked about but rejected because Kim simply did not have the money.

The mediator asked what was the value of peace of mind; Kim replied 250 dollars, because that was all she had. The mediator asked if he could tell the plaintiff – the answer was affirmative, but only if they agreed to drop the case completely. Kim was worried that if she paid them, then they were unable to find a new girl, that they would start all over again.

3rd plaintiff caucus
During the mediator's absence the plaintiffs had jointly agreed that they would accept the offer of 150 dollars. The mediator asked if they were prepared to drop the case completely and this was agreed. The mediator then announced that agreement had been reached and that he would inform the defendant.

He then left the room to tell Kim they would accept the 150 dollars. She was naturally delighted; the mediator had to explain that the plaintiff had agreed to accept the old offer before he had had a chance to relay the new one.

The mediator then called both parties together and a cheque was handed over.

Comment: This was a particularly difficult mediation, because neither side had the benefit of legal advice, and although the mediator was a lawyer, he could not give either side advice himself. A further complication was the imbalance of power, although this was somewhat lessened by the fact that not all the plaintiffs could agree with each other. This was the reason why the mediator did not immediately float the latest offer, but waited to see what had transpired while he was out of the room.

IV. PERSONAL INJURY MEDIATION APRIL 1989

The Plaintiff was a young man of 27 who had been the passenger in an open topped sports car. The driver of the car lost control of the vehicle which hit the curb and overturned, throwing the passenger out. The passenger sustained a dislocated shoulder and scarring to his back from sliding along the surface of the road. He was taken to hospital, where road grit was removed from his back and shoulder. Small amounts of tar were unable to be removed however and he was left with a series of grey scars on his back.

He was unemployed at the time of the accident, but some six weeks later obtained a job as a pipe fitter, as his shoulder had fully recovered.

He was claiming $300,000 compensation from the driver of the car, who was fully covered by an insurance policy, up to a limit of $300,000. A medical estimate had been obtained stating that plastic surgery was possible and would cost around $10,000.

The mediation had been instigated by the insurance company, who had offered $30,000 compensation.

The Plaintiff and his lawyer arrived 30 minutes late for the mediation and offered no apology.

After having made his opening statement, the mediator requested that the plaintiff's lawyer outline his case. The lawyer was badly prepared and spent 30 minutes reading previous correspondence to the insurance company in the wrong chronological order. He finally asked the plaintiff to remove his shirt in order to show the physical evidence, first having requested that one of the insurance company representatives (female) leave the room. The crux of his case was that his client was so embarrassed by the scars that he could never again take his shirt off in public, and could therefore never again go swimming or take a holiday on the beach. The lawyer further claimed in extremely colourful language that he considered the insurance company's offer so derisory that he would be asking for triple damages to be awarded in this case, ie $900,000.

The insurance company then stated their case, pointing out that since leaving hospital the plaintiff had had no further treatment and that in his opinion there was no permanent scarring. They also pointed out that the case was only six months old, and the level of scarring now was not of the same proportion as that described in a most extravagant way by the lawyer.

1st caucus with the plaintiff
The lawyer again pointed out that in his opinion he would get triple damages due to the low offer made by the insurance company, bearing in mind his client had a 40-year life span ahead of him, during which he could not take his shirt off.

When questioned by the mediator he could see no weaknesses in his case whatsoever, and therefore refused to move from his position on the $300,000.

1st caucus with the defence
They pointed out that having seen the physical evidence, they ought to reduce their offer. They stated that the plaintiffs case was laughable and that although they saw no reason to continue, in order to play the game, they would offer a further $5,000 if it would settle the case.

2nd caucus with the plaintiff
On being told of the extra $5,000, the lawyer started to leave, shouting that this was proof of 'bad faith' by the insurance company. Having been calmed down by the mediator, the lawyer then proposed his client should get a pension for life.

At this point the mediation was terminated by the mediator. As a final shot he invited both parties to make a 5-minute presentation of the facts in a further joint session. This having been done the insurance company left.

Following the mediation the lawyer stated that he had expected the mediator to make a ruling on the case, and that he would in fact have accepted quote 'about 100,000 dollars', it also transpired that he had never taken a case like this to trial before.

Comments: This mediation did not work for a number of reasons. The plaintiff's lawyer was extremely aggressive, ill prepared and inexperienced. His case was extremely weak, but he would not accept that. His position was that because the driver was insured for $300,000, then that would be the settlement point, and anything lower was bad faith by the insurance company. He was so inexperienced that he did not know the risks in taking this case to trial. Mediation can only work if both parties genuinely want a settlement. In this case it was only the insurance company who were prepared to settle.

V. MOTOR VEHICLE ACCIDENT APRIL 1989

This case involved two motor vehicles, one driven by an elderly man, the defendant, who it was claimed had driven straight across an intersection rather than make a mandatory left turn. His car was hit by the plaintiff. She admitted to being 10mph over the speed limit, but claimed he went straight across in front of her. Both parties were taken to hospital, the old gentleman being in a confused state and admitting he was in the wrong. The lady driver sustained neck and back injuries and was off work for 13 weeks.

Following the standard mediator opening statement, both parties stated their case. They were both well prepared, having photographic evidence of both the accident site and the vehicles. A claim of $20,000 had been made and an offer tendered of $5,200.

1st plaintiff caucus
The evidence was looked at and the mediator asked the plaintiff lawyer how he had arrived at his valuation. When the figures were added up, he immediately dropped his claim to $15,000.

1st defence caucus
The mediator revealed that the claim was down to $15,000. He then asked how the defence valued the case. The figures added up to $13,000, at which point the issue of percentage liability arose. The defence claimed 60-40 and therefore increased its offer to $7,100. The upper end of the value would have been $7,800.

2nd plaintiff caucus
The mediator stated that both sides actually agreed on the valuation of the case and that the defence thought 60-40 on liability due to the speed of the lady driver. Hence an offer of $7,100. The plaintiff countered with a claim of $10,000.

2nd defence caucus
The mediator pointed out that the case was only six months old, and that the longer it went on the more chance there was of the plaintiff suffering more back trouble and the case becoming more expensive. At this point the defence proposed to split the difference, to increase the offer to $8,750. It also transpired that $2,000 had already been paid out in medical bills.

3rd plaintiff caucus
The mediator didn't give the figure immediately, but explained the current positions. He clarified that $2,000 had indeed already been paid and then pointed out that the defence had in fact offered $10,750, being the current $8,750 plus the earlier $2,000. He suggested that the plaintiff had therefore got a settlement $750 higher than they had requested. They agreed.

The mediator then called both sides together, announced the settlement and congratulated the parties on what they had achieved.

VI. COMPANY MEDIATION MAY 1989 (UK)

The father was in his early 70's and had run the company successfully for the last 25 years. He had one daughter, and his wife was deceased. Through a trust the daughter was beneficial owner of 51 per cent of the company with the father controlling the balance. However, the father effectively controlled 100 per cent of the voting rights of the company because the trustees were all contemporaries and associates and they had a history of respecting his wishes.

The daughter was on the Board of Directors of the company, essentially watching out for her interest. The daughter was not, however, very interested in the company or in business in general and there was little possibility that she could succeed in running the business on the death of the father.

For certain reasons there was a falling out between father and daughter over her performance as a Director and the father wished her to resign. She refused, and the father was on the verge of calling a general meeting of shareholders for the purpose of having her voted out as a director, when they went into mediation.

Father and daughter had not spoken for several months and there had recently been acrimonious exchanges of correspondence. The mediation session was the first time they were able to discuss the problem face-to-face.

In the course of the mediation it transpired that the daughter did not really want to remain on the Board but she was unwilling to resign for several reasons:

(i) she was concerned that her father would not properly plan for a successor in management and the business would fail causing the loss of her interest which she was hoping would provide her with substantial capital in coming years,

(ii) she wanted to continue to receive information about the company so that she could monitor this succession problem;

(iii) her financial condition required her to continue to receive directors' fees, and

(iv) she was worried that the trustees might alter her position as a beneficiary under the trust if she was no longer involved with the business.

The father on the other hand, did not really want to have the daughter removed as a director because he feared that this would create a permanent emotional break with the daughter and be the source of personal embarrassment.

The dispute was successfully resolved over 6 hours of mediation by:

(i) The daughter resigning from the Board,
(ii) The father
   – agreeing to give the daughter personally from his own resources the director's fees she would be losing.
   – agreeing to keep the daughter informed on his succession plans and keep her generally informed about the business.
   – agreeing to speak to the trustees and express his wish that there be no change in the beneficial interest of the daughter in the business prior to or after his death.

Comments: This is a good example of a dispute which was not suitable for litigation because the parties wished to resolve their dispute in private and the final mutually satisfactory result was one which a court would have been unable to order.

VII. PARTNERSHIP DISPUTE MARCH 1990

Mediation can be a very effective method for the resolution of partnership disputes. Partnership disputes are not dissimilar to divorces. They can become intensely personal and emotional and often the parties become unable to agree upon even the smallest details.

In the business context partnership disputes can be very damaging. Obviously two of the most important features of a successful business are leadership and general management. When partners are fighting, the business must inevitably suffer; staff and client loyalties will be partisanly called upon, senior management time will be spent on the conflict rather than the business, and there will be an internal loss of morale, confidence and stability. Unless the dispute is resolved quickly, there is a very real chance that the business itself will fail.

There are many types of partnership disputes. This recent case was the successful dissolution of a partnership through mediation which resulted in preserving the business for the continuing partner while permitting the departing partner to obtain what he considered to be a satisfactory return for his investment.

The partnership, in the form of a limited liability company, was owned 60 per cent by the senior partner and 40 per cent by the junior partner. Their business was in the service sector in London and each partner had an excellent reputation in their field and a significant client following. They were supported in their efforts by several associates and clerical staff.

The senior partner was approaching retirement and wished to resolve all partnership matters over the period of several months and then effectively dissolve the partnership. The junior partner wished to continue in the business and to maintain as much of the existing infrastructure as he could support on his own or with other partners whom he might bring into the business.

Several years earlier the partners had entered into a partnership agreement which set the terms and conditions for exactly this situation – the 'retirement buy-out' of the senior partner. These terms and conditions were considered fair and equitable by the parties when this agreement was entered into but during the period between execution of the agreement and the beginning of the negotiations to dissolve the partnership certain events had occurred which called into question these fundamental terms and conditions.

Under the agreement the buy-out price was to be based upon the greater of (I) a certain multiple of net asset value or (II) a certain multiple of the average net profits of the company over the three years prior to the sale. However during the interim period between this agreement and the negotiations, in fact only a few months before the negotiation began, a major company in their field had made an offer to purchase the entire partnership at a price far in excess of that envisaged by the agreement.

The senior partner wanted to accept this offer but the junior partner vetoed it and the opportunity was lost. The junior partner justified his decision on the basis that he preferred the independence which the smaller partnership gave him and in the long run he felt that he could do better financially running his own business than in being part of a larger operation.

The senior partner, looking forward to retirement, felt that he had suffered a grave loss as a result of this decision and now considered that if the junior partner was going to buy him out, the price should be based upon the higher value offered by the third party, not the price calculated according to existing partnership agreement. The gap was large and the junior partner could not financially bridge it.

The initial stages of the negotiation were difficult. The senior partner fixed his position to the full amount which he would have received from the third party and the junior partner discounted the value of the business down to zero—polarisation and the business began to suffer. The staff were aware that some changes were in the offing but they did not know what they would be and the partners, who by then could no longer effectively negotiate face-to-face, began to spend their fee-earning time considering what legal steps they could take to improve their bargaining positions. Finally the lawyer acting for one of the partners suggested mediation.

The mediation was carried out in two sessions. The first session of five hours was held in a suite at a London hotel. During this mediation session, which involved both joint and private meetings, many of the emotional aspects came out. It soon became apparent why the two partners were personally not suited to negotiate with each other, and near the end the partners and the mediator succeeded in focusing on the practical problems of a settlement.

At the close of the first session the partners drew up a time-table for further meetings and a check list, with responsibilities, for further information which they needed to continue their negotiations.

Approximately one month later the second mediation session was held in the partners' offices. This session lasted less than two hours and was conducted almost entirely in a joint meeting, with the mediator intervening only when they were not able to agree quickly on a particular point.

The final price was obviously a key issue and the mediator used the 'set aside' technique, holding this one back until all other issues had been agreed. Then when the parties were still separated on price, although the gap was narrowed to less than 10 per cent of what had existed before the mediation process had begun, the mediator uncovered a new issue which permitted the seller to achieve something of value but did not increase the cost to the purchaser and the deadlock was broken. Both partners were able to walk away preserving their relationship and the business.

VIII CONSTRUCTION MEDIATION JUNE 1990

In 1988 a well-known shoe manufacturer filed a claim in the High Court against five parties claiming £400,000 in damages resulting from allegedly negligent workmanship, design and supervision of their prestigious new factory. The original five defendants in the action were the architects, the supervising consultant, the design engineers, the main contractor and the electrical sub-contractors.

The factory had been completed some four years prior to the filing of the claim but problems soon developed with the factory lighting, heating and ventilation system, and the main electrical supply capacity. Remedial works were carried out by the electrical sub-contractor at a cost of £60,000 but these works failed to rectify the problems.

In May 1990, after direct negotiations had failed and only two weeks before the anticipated seven-to-twelve week trial was due to begin, the insurer for one of the defendants asked IDR Europe to arrange a mediation. With the agreement of all parties and their solicitors the mediation was convened on very short notice at a London hotel.

At this stage there were only four defendants left in the case. The architects had been released from the action by the plaintiff two days before the mediation began. The mechanical sub-contractors had actually gone into liquidation during the course of the construction and had not even been made a party to the claim.

As to the remaining four defendants:

— The electrical sub-contractors were not insured and would have gone bankrupt simply from having to carry the legal costs of defending themselves,
— The design engineers were insured and their insurers had paid £250,000, the limit of their indemnity, into a sinking fund which would have been substantially reduced by the defence costs in a trial.
— The supervising consultant was partially insured but claimed that the fault and liability belonged to the design engineers.

— The main contractors were caught in the cross-fire between the design engineers and the other parties, but they were prepared to participate financially in a settlement in order to avoid the costs of the trial.

The mediation was conducted in two parts: a mediation session of one day followed by continued mediation by telephone and facsimile. During the course of the mediation session there were several meetings among all the parties which produced the 'venting of frustration' which is an integral part of all successful mediations. The parties then moved on in separate private meetings to analyse carefully their respective positions and the day closed with a firm offer being put on the table by the defendants.

Over the next few days the mediation continued with regular communications between the mediator and the parties, utilising detailed cost/benefit estimates relating to anticipated results of the trial should the dispute have been allowed to reach that stage. These efforts resulted in a substantial cash settlement acceptable to all the parties several days before the scheduled trial date and established once again the power of the mediator — a neutral party — to bring the parties to an agreement when direct negotiations have failed and the only alternative seems to be litigation. Impressed with the power of the mediation process and the results which can be achieved, a solicitor for one of the parties asked to be trained as a mediator and solicitors for another party expressed their willingness to have more disputes resolved in this manner.

United States Arbitration & Mediation of Arizona, Nevada & New Mexico Inc. – Rules of Arbitration

1. Rules

The parties to a dispute shall be deemed to have made these rules a part of their agreement to arbitrate and shall be legally bound to comply with these rules.

2. Conduct of Proceedings

One or both parties to a dispute should contact United States Arbitration and Mediation ('USA&M') and furnish the names and addresses of all parties and a brief description of the dispute. Each party is then sent explanatory materials and preliminary documents. USA&M provides the parties with a method to select an arbitrator (see Rule 4), USA&M estimates the length of the hearing (see Rule 7) and estimated fees are collected from the parties (see Rule 6). Thereafter, the case is turned over to the arbitrator who sets up the time and place of the hearing, conducts the hearing and renders an award.

Upon receipt of the case, the arbitrator has broad authority to conduct the arbitration process in any manner deemed reasonable to reach a just determination. This includes the authority to order a party to answer reasonable written questions, testify under oath, or produce documents prior to the hearing. The arbitrator shall be the judge of the admissibility of the evidence offered by the parties, and conformity to legal rules of evidence shall not be necessary. The arbitrator may receive and consider witness affidavits, but shall give them only such weight as the arbitrator deems appropriate. The arbitrator has authority to settle all points of controversy in the dispute and award appropriate relief. State law allows arbitration awards to be enforced like civil court judgments and establishes specific procedures to follow to enforce an award.

All arbitration proceedings are confidential to the extent allowed by law and desired by the parties.

3. Initiating arbitration under specific language in contract, lease, etc.

A party wishing to initiate arbitration in accordance with a provision in a contract, lease, etc, calling for arbitration should contact USA&M. The initiating party should also give notice, as required by the contract, to the other party. The other party shall have the opportunity to respond to such notice and the arbitration process will proceed as in Rule 2 above.

4. Selection of Arbitrators

Unless the parties agree otherwise only one arbitrator is to be assigned to each case. The parties will be sent lists of arbitrators from which they make their selection. Parties are urged to agree to a particular arbitrator, but if they cannot, parties cross off any listed arbitrator they feel is unacceptable and attach a numerical preference to the remaining arbitrators. Parties may not cross off more than one half of the number of arbitrators on the list. The actual arbitrator picked to arbitrate the dispute is to be the arbitrator with the lowest total preference points who agrees to accept the case. In the event of a tie in preference points, USA&M will select the arbitrator from those remaining.

If a three member panel of arbitrators is requested, the parties shall each select an arbitrator. The selected arbitrators will then select a third arbitrator in accordance with the above-described method. The third arbitrator shall be the 'lead' arbitrator.

The lists of arbitrators to be sent to the parties are to be compiled by USA&M using the background information supplied by the arbitrators and considering the nature and locality of the dispute involved. USA&M may impose a time limit for the parties to return the selection sheets, and if a party fails to make a selection, the party will be deemed to have no preference as to the list of arbitrators.

5. Arbitrator

Arbitrators are independent contractors and not agents or employees of USA&M.

Arbitrators and USA&M are entitled to a qualified 'good faith' immunity from suit.

6. The amount and collection of fees

USA&M charges an administrative fee for its services. The amount of this fee is set by USA&M's fee schedule in effect at the time of initiating arbitration. This fee schedule may be changed without notice.

Arbitrators charge on an hourly basis. Arbitrators are entitled to compensation for any time they spend on the case, including time for such activities as the arbitration hearing, legal research, travel and deliberations. Arbitrators are also entitled to compensation for any costs they incur, such as telephone or travel expenses.

USA&M estimates the amount of arbitrator time involved in a case and collects estimated arbitrator's fees in advance of the case being turned over to the selected arbitrator. Such estimated fees are placed in USA&M's trust account. At the conclusion of the arbitration proceedings, the arbitrator executes a 'Time Spent– Services Rendered' affidavit setting out how much arbitrator time was involved in the proceedings and any costs. If the amount of time actually spent is more than the estimated time, the parties are responsible to pay to USA&M any extra monies owing. Where appropriate, the arbitrator may order additional estimated fees to be paid into USA&M and the award may be withheld pending such payment.

Unless the parties agree otherwise, each party is responsible for paying a proportionate share of USA&M's fees and any arbitrator's fee, with the arbitrator having the ability to assess, as part of the award, all or part of the total fees of the arbitration proceeding against any party.

Unless the parties agree otherwise, **when an arbitration is initiated under an arbitration clause in a contract, lease, etc**, and the non-initiating party simply denies the claim, the initiating party is responsible for the total fees and costs of the arbitration, with the arbitrator having the ability to assess, as part of the award, all or part of the total costs and fees of the arbitration proceeding against any party.

If for any reason the parties do not proceed to arbitration after paying arbitration fees, USA&M is entitled to a full administrative fee. Arbitrators are also entitled to fees for any time they may have spent on the case.

7. Determination of length of hearing

Based on documentation received and any conversations with the parties, USA&M determines the approximate length of the arbitration hearing. The arbitrator shall have, full authority to determine the actual length of the arbitration, the relevancy of testimony and evidence, the need for site inspections, the need for pre-hearing discovery, motions, etc.

8. Failure to proceed

Whenever an arbitration clause, an arbitration contract, or these rules call for a party to proceed with arbitration, a party shall be deemed to have failed to proceed with arbitration when (1) the party repeatedly fails to respond to communications from USA&M, or (2) fails to proceed to the next step of arbitration after being properly informed to so proceed, or (3) fails to comply with an arbitrator's order, or (4) otherwise indicates an intent not to proceed, USA&M or the arbitrator will determine when a party has 'failed to proceed'.

An arbitration award shall not be made solely on the default of a party, but such an award may be made in the absence of a party upon a proper showing by the other party(s).

9. Waiver of rules or applicable laws

Any party who proceeds with the arbitration after knowledge that any provision or requirement of these rules or any applicable laws has not been complied with and who fails to object thereto, waives any right to object later.

10. Rules may be amended or modified

These rules may be amended or modified by USA&M at any time without notice.

11. Matters not addressed and authority of USA&M

Any of the above procedures may be altered by USA&M to fit the circumstances of a particular case. Any matter not specifically addressed by these rules, or any conflict or ambiguity in these rules, will be decided by USA&M in a manner designed to result in a full, fair and impartial arbitration proceeding. USA&M has authority to prepare forms, resolve procedural disputes, impose time limits on the parties, and otherwise require a party to take action or refrain from taking action.

Neither USA&M nor the arbitrator is a necessary party in any judicial proceedings related to the arbitration.

ADR Net Members (November 1991)

Andrew M Jackson & Co.
Victoria Chambers
Bowlalley Lane
Hull HU1 1XY
Tel: 0482 25242
Contact: David Dunk

Anstey Sargent & Probert
4, 5 & 6 Barnfield Crescent
Exeter
Devon EX1 1RF
Tel: 0392 411221
Contact: Jeremy Robinson

Barlows
117A Guildford Street
Chertsey
Surrey KT16 9AF
Tel: 0932 568245
Contact: Michael England

Birkett, Westhorp & Long
Essex House
42 Crouch Street
Colchester
Essex CO3 3HH
Tel: 0206 562296
Contact: Adrian Livesley

Elliott & Co.
Centurion House
Deansgate
Manchester M3 3WT
Tel: 061-834 9933
Contact: Geoff Lord

Humphries Kirk
4 Rempstone Road
Swanage
Dorset BH19 1DP
Tel: 0929 423301
Contact: Michael Greenleaves

Hunt Dickins
Express Buildings
17-29 Upper Parliament Street
Nottingham NG1 2AQ
Tel: 0602 350350
Contact: Euan Temple

Jacksons
7/15 Queen's Square
Middlesbrough
Cleveland TS2 1AL
Tel: 0642 244154
Contact: Robin Bloom

Knight & Sons
31 Ironmarket
Newcastle-under-Lyme
Staffordshire ST5 1RL
Tel: 0782 619225
Contact: Derek Miller

Ledingham Chalmers
1 Golden Square
Aberdeen AB9 1HA
Tel: 0224 647344
Contact: Peter Sharp

Lewis Silkin
1 Butler Place
Buckingham Gate
London SW1H 0PT
Tel: 071-222 8191
Contact: Tom Coates

Linnells
12 King Edward Street
Oxford OX1 4HX
Tel: 0865 248607
Contact:
Jonathan Lloyd-Jones

McGrigor Donald
Pacific House
70 Wellington Street
Glasgow G2 6SB
Tel: 041-248 6677
Contact: Vincent Connor

Maurice Putsman & Co.
Britannia House
50 Great Charles Street
Birmingham B3 2LT
Tel: 021-236 9116/0
Contact: Sarah Ferdinand

Morgan Bruce
Bradley Court
Park Place
Cardiff CF1 3DP
Tel: 0222 233677
Contact:
Phillip Howell-Richardson

Pinsent & Co.
Post & Mail House
26 Colmore Circus
Birmingham B4 6BH
Tel: 021-200 1050
Contact: Andrew Paton

Simpson Curtis
41 Park Square
Leeds LS1 2EX
Tel: 0532 433433
Contact: Michael James

Simpson & Marwick
18 Heriot Row
Edinburgh EH3 6HS
Tel: 031-557 1545
Contact: Douglas Russell

Veale Wasbrough
Orchard Court
Orchard Lane
Bristol BS1 5DS
Tel: 0272 252020
Contact: Roger Hoyle

Ringrose Wharton & Co.
Equity & Law Building
30–34 Baldwin Street
Bristol BS1 1NR
Tel: 0272 226233
Contact: Robert Wharton

Draft ADR Contract Clauses

INTRODUCTION

Benefits of an ADR clause

(1) Valuable where the parties in dispute wish to maintain a continuing relationship, particularly in the fields of construction, joint ventures, information technology supply, franchises and distribution and agency.

(2) Enables/obliges the parties to consider ADR.

(3) Enables senior management to be involved at an earlier stage of a dispute.

(4) Flexible – voluntary, lots of alternatives.

Cautionary notes

1. The simple, non-binding clause
Cannot do any harm, but parties may not be able to agree on procedure and could be used as an excuse for time-wasting.

2. Simple clause making non-binding ADR obligatory
Could be used for time-wasting. It does not prevent the parties from ultimately going to court for final or interim relief. It is dependent on willing parties and advisers and on immediate help from CEDR.

3. Clause with some procedures and obligatory, non-binding ADR
Helps parties to start ADR, but creates chances for more time-wasting. Procedures may be inappropriate for the dispute when it arises. Interim relief is not excluded.

4. A few points to consider
(a) Whether to allow ADR to begin before written statements are exchanged
  (b) Whether to involve senior executives
  (c) How long to allow for agreement over the ADR process
  (d) How long to allow the ADR procedure to run
  (e) Whether to provide for an advisory opinion from the neutral
  (f) Whether to include disincentives to litigation
  (g) Whether to require notice of intent to litigate

SAMPLE CLAUSE FROM DIGITAL EQUIPMENT

The agreement will be governed by the laws of England. The parties will, with the help of the Centre for Dispute Resolution, London, attempt to resolve disputes by means of alternative dispute resolution. Failing resolution any dispute arising out of or in connection with this agreement, including any question regarding its existence, validity or termination, shall be referred to and finally resolved by arbitration under the rules of the London Court of International Arbitration, which rules are deemed to be incorporated by reference into this clause.

SAMPLE CLAUSE FROM TURNER KENNETH BROWN

Any dispute which may arise between the parties concerning this Agreement may with the agreement of all relevant parties be submitted for resolution utilising alternative dispute resolution techniques including without limitation such techniques as conciliation, mediation, the the 'mini-trial' or 'executive tribunal'. If such techniques are considered by the parties to be appropriate to resolve the dispute they shall consult the Centre for Dispute Resolution to advise upon the most appropriate procedure and the appointment of suitably qualified personnel.

Nothing in the above clause shall prevent either party from seeking appropriate relief from the English Courts at any time and the parties hereby submit to the non-exclusive jurisdiction of those Courts for such purpose. For the avoidance of doubt this shall include the right for either party to make application for (ex-parte) interlocutory injunctive or other relief should it consider this appropriate.

The construction performance and validity of this Agreement shall in all respects be governed by the laws of England.

SAMPLE CLAUSE FROM CEDR

The parties will attempt in good faith to resolve any disputes or claim arising out of or relating to this agreement promptly by negotiations between senior executives of the parties who have authority to settle the dispute.

If the matter is not resolved through negotiation, the parties will attempt in good faith to resolve the dispute through a procedure such as mediation or executive tribunal or other dispute resolution technique recommended from time to time by the Centre for Dispute Resolution of London ('CEDR'). If the parties need advice in appointing a suitable neutral and in formulating the appropriate procedure they can seek assistance from CEDR.

If the matter has not been resolved by such a procedure within [. . . . .] days of its initiation or if either party will not participate in such procedure, the dispute shall be referred to [arbitration in accordance with . . . .] [litigation].

SAMPLE CLAUSE FROM R.C. I'ANSON BANKS

ADR and arbitration

26. If during the continuance of the Partnership or at any time thereafter any dispute difference or question shall arise between the Partners (or former Partners) or any of them or any of their respective representatives or between any Partner (or former Partner) and the representatives of any other Partner (or former Partner) touching the Partnership or the accounts dealings or transactions thereof or the dissolution or winding up thereof or the construction meaning or effect of this Deed or anything herein contained or the rights or liabilities of the Partners (or former Partners) or their respective representatives hereunder or otherwise howsoever then and in such event:

(a) the parties to such dispute difference or question shall forthwith attempt to resolve the same by negotiation;

(b) if such dispute difference or question shall not be resolved within [. . .] days the parties thereto shall forthwith attempt to resolve the same by such dispute resolution procedure conducted in such manner and with the assistance of such indpendent person as shall be agreed between them or in default of agreement recommended by the [Centre for Dispute Resolution OR the Chartered Institute of Arbitrators OR the British Academy of Experts]

(c) if such dispute difference or question shall not be resolved within [. . .] days after the expiration of the period specified in sub-clauses (b) hereof or if one or more of the parties thereto shall be unwilling to participate in any form of dispute resolution procedure the same shall be referred to a single arbitrator to be agreed upon by the parties and in default of agreement to be nominated by the President OR Chairman of the [. . .] in accordance with and subject to the provisions of the Arbitration Acts 1950 to 1979.

Provided Always that for the avoidance of doubt it is hereby agreed and declared that:

(i) each party shall as regards any attempt to resolve such dispute difference or question pursuant to sub-clause (a) or (b) hereof be subject to the like obligation as is referred to in clause 16(3) hereof.

(ii) any arbitrator shall have full power to dissolve the partnership if he shall think fit.

Commentary

Variation 2: Alternative dispute resolution

So-called ADR techniques, i.e. conciliation, mediation and the 'mini-trial' or 'executive tribunal', are recent imports from the United States of America and seem ideally suited to the resolution of partnership disputes. At the same time, their consensual nature precludes anything in the nature of a specifically enforceable agreement to resort thereto, hence the deliberate use of the word 'attempt' in sub-clause (b) and the recognition that one partner may, for whatever reason, refuse to co-operate; see sub-clause (c). It would, of course, be pointless to force an unwilling partner to 'go through the motions' of the ADR process. Equally, it might be argued that the inclusion of an express reference to ADR in the agreement is unnecessary, since such procedures can be invoked at any stage, even whilst an arbitration is continuing. It is, however, the editor's view that such are the potential advantages of ADR, particularly if the procedure is initiated before a potential dispute has fully developed, that a clause in this form will ensure that this option is not overlooked.

The three bodies named at the end of sub-clause (b) are all co-operating in the task of promoting the use of ADR in the English legal system and can assist partners by recommending particular ADR techniques as well the names of potential mediators or 'neutrals'.

ADR is dependent on the good faith of the participants and it is, perhaps, appropriate to underline this fact by including proviso (a).

Center for Public Resources, New York – Sample ADR Clauses for Business Contracts (October 1990)

INTRODUCTION

The basic theory of predispute ADR agreements is simple: Be prepared. When drafting a contract, lawyers and business executives should include procedures they can turn to in the event of a future dispute. Better to construct such processes when the parties are feeling co-operative, optimistic and enthusiastic, the notion goes, than when they are suspicious, tense, angry and mired in a messy disagreement.

Alternatives has frequently reported on adherents of this view. In our June 1990 issue, for instance, a Canadian lawyer argued forcefully for the importance of using such clauses in computer contracts. And readers of our January 1988 edition learned that General Mills Inc., a sustaining member of the CPR Legal Program, will not sign contracts with companies that spurn these clauses. (These and many other examples of ADR contract clause usage, along with analysis of and commentary on clause construction, enforceability, and so on, can be found in *CPR Practice Guide: Crafting ADR Contract Clauses*. The guide, an extensive, nuts-and-bolts manual, is available from CPR at the address and telephone listed below.)

The CPR Legal Program, a pioneering promoter of these predispute ADR agreements, is gratified at the growing interest in and use of them. And to spur this development further along, CPR has composed three sample ADR contract clauses. They are presented below.

Unlike standard arbitration clauses, these CPR-crafted clauses generally contemplate (1) use of non-binding ADR processes and, if they fail, (2) resort to a binding decision through arbitration or litigation. The thought behind this preference for a non-binding process followed, in the event of failure, by a binding award is that consensual settlements are superior to imposed decisions. With the former, parties can flex their creativity, preserve friendly relations and control their fates much better than with the latter, CPR believes.

Within this general framework, the CPR sample clauses vary somewhat. The three-step clause calls for negotiations between senior executives when a dispute first flares. If those talks do not succeed, the parties proceed to a non-binding minitrial or mediation. If this second stage also fails, the clause anticipates a third and final step – binding decision by an arbitrator or arbitrators.

CPR's four-step ADR clause features two stages of negotiation rather than one, as in the three-step clause. In the first stage, the project managers, who are named in the clause, try to negotiate a resolution. If they fail, senior executives try their hand at settlement negotiation. If their talks also prove fruitless, the parties proceed to a mini-trial or mediation. Finally, if none of these three non-binding processes succeeds in resolving the matter, the four-step clause anticipates either arbitration or litigation at the parties' election.

The two-step ADR clause is simpler than the other two. It contemplates either mediation or a mini-trial, followed by either arbitration or litigation.

Other things being equal, CPR favors the three-step clause. The sequence of presentation below reflects that preference. There may, however, be disputes for which one of the other sample clauses seems best. In any case, CPR encourages parties to customize these clauses for the matter at hand.

The three sample clauses incorporate, by reference, CPR's model rules for the conduct of mediations, mini-trials and arbitrations. These model rules — which also encourage modification for particular cases — were drawn up over the past several years by committees of expert attorneys. The models are available from CPR (at the address in Appendix 10) and have been published in *Alternatives* as well. (Mediation — April 1986 at p.1, Mini-trial — July 1989 at p.109; Arbitration — September 1989 at p.149.)

The sample clauses also incorporate, by reference, CPR's panels of ADR neutrals. These panel lists are available from CPR and were published in the March 1990 *Alternatives*, at p.48. CPR also assists disputants in selecting ADR neutrals.

THREE-STEP DISPUTE RESOLUTION CLAUSE

Negotiation — Mediation — Arbitration
The parties will attempt in good faith to resolve any controversy or claim arising out of or relating to this agreement promptly by negotiations between senior executives of the parties who have authority to settle the controversy (and who do not have direct responsibility for administration of this agreement).

The disputing party shall give the other party written notice of the dispute. Within twenty days after receipt of said notice, the receiving party shall submit to the other a written response. The notice and response shall include (a) a statement of each party's position and a summary of the evidence and arguments supporting its position, and (b) the name and title of the executive who will represent that party. The executives shall meet at a mutually acceptable time and place within thirty days of the date of the disputing party's notice and thereafter as often as they reasonably deem necessary to exchange relevant information and to attempt to resolve the dispute.

If the matter has not been resolved within sixty days of the disputing party's notice, or if the party receiving said notice will not meet within thirty days, either party may initiate mediation of the controversy or claim in accordance with the Center for Public Resources Model Procedure for Mediation of Business Disputes.

If the matter has not been resolved pursuant to the aforesaid mediation procedure within sixty days of the initiation of such procedure, or if either party will not participate in a mediation, the controversy shall be settled by arbitration in accordance with the Center for Public Resources Rules for Non-Administered Arbitration of Business Disputes, by (a sole arbitrator) (three arbitrators, of whom each party shall appoint one) (three arbitrators, none of whom shall be appointed by either party). (Any mediator or arbitrator not appointed by a party shall be selected from the CPR Panels of Distinguished Neutrals.) The arbitration shall be governed by the United States Arbitration Act, 9 U.S.C. § 1-16, and judgment upon the award rendered by the Arbitrator(s) may be entered by any court having jurisdiction thereof. The place of arbitration shall be _____ The arbitrator(s) (are) (are not) empowered to award damages in excess of actual damages, including punitive damages.

All deadlines specified in this Article 00 may be extended by mutual agreement.

The procedures specified in this Article 00 shall be the sole and exclusive procedures for the resolution of disputes between the parties arising out of or relating to this agreement, provided, however, that a party may seek a preliminary injunction or other preliminary judicial relief if in its judgment such action is necessary to avoid irreparable damage. Despite such action the parties will continue to participate in good faith in the procedures specified in this Article 00. All applicable statutes of limitation shall be tolled while the procedures specified in this Article 00 are pending. The parties will take such action, if any, required to effectuate such tolling.

Note: Mediation frequently results in a resolution even when unfacilitated negotiations did not; however, if the parties prefer, the mediation step may be omitted. Moreover, the Center for Public Resources Model Mini-trial Procedure may be substituted for the mediation procedure. 90-120 days would be a reasonable period for this procedure.

FOUR-STEP DISPUTE RESOLUTION CLAUSE

Dual Negotiation — Mediation — Arbitration or Litigation
The parties will attempt in good faith to resolve any controversy or claim arising out of or relating to this agreement promptly by negotiations between executives of the parties.

If a controversy or claim should arise, _____
of X Co. and _____ of Y Co,
or their respective successors in the positions they now hold (herein called the 'project managers'), will meet at least once and will attempt to resolve the matter. Either project manager may request the other to meet within fourteen days, at a mutually agreed time and place.

If the matter has not been resolved within twenty days of their first meeting, the project managers shall refer the matter to senior executives, who shall have authority to settle the dispute (herein called 'the senior executives'). Thereupon, the project managers shall promptly prepare and exchange memoranda stating the issues in dispute and their positions, summarizing the negotiations which have taken place and attaching relevant documents. The senior executives will meet for negotiations within fourteen days of the end of the twenty-day period referred to above, at a mutually agreed time and place.

If the matter has not been resolved within thirty days of the meeting of the senior executives, the parties will attempt in good faith to resolve the controversy or claim in accordance with the Center for Public Resources Model Procedure for Mediation of Business Disputes.

If the matter has not been resolved pursuant to the aforesaid mediation procedures within sixty days of the commencement of such procedure, or if either party will not participate in mediation,

(Select one of the following alternatives)

(i) the controversy shall be settled by arbitration in accordance with the Center for Public Resources Rules for Non-Administered Arbitration of Business Disputes, by (a sole arbitrator) (three arbitrators, of whom each party shall appoint one) (three arbitrators, none of whom shall be appointed by either party). (Any mediator or arbitrator not appointed by a party shall be selected from the CPR Panels of Distinguished Neutrals). The arbitration shall be governed by the United States Arbitration Act, 9 U.S.C. § 1-16, and judgment upon the award rendered by the Arbitrator(s) may be entered by any court having jurisdiction thereof. The place of arbitration shall be _____. The arbitrator(s) (are) (are not) empowered to award damages in excess of actual damages, including punitive damages.

(ii) either party may initiate litigation (upon 00 days' written notice to the other party).

All deadlines specified in this Article 00 may be extended by mutual agreement.

The procedures specified in this Article 00 shall be the sole and exclusive procedures for the resolution of disputes between the parties arising out of or relating to this agreement; provided, however, that a party may seek a preliminary injunction or other preliminary judicial relief if in its judgment such action is necessary to avoid irreparable damage. Despite such action the parties will continue to participate in good faith in the procedures specified in this Article 00. All applicable statutes of limitation shall be tolled while the procedures specified in this Article 00 are pending. The parties will take such action, if any, required to effectuate such tolling.

Note. Mediation frequently results in a resolution even when unfacilitated negotiations did not; however, if the parties prefer, the mediation step may be omitted. Moreover, the Center for Public Resources Model Mini-trial Procedure may be substituted for the mediation procedure. 90-120 days would be a reasonable period for this procedure.

TWO-STEP DISPUTE RESOLUTION CLAUSE

Mediation − Arbitration or Litigation

The parties will attempt in good faith to resolve any controversy or claim arising out of or relating to this agreement by mediation in accordance with the Center for Public Resources Model Procedure for Mediation of Business Disputes.**

If the matter has not been resolved pursuant to the aforesaid mediation procedure within sixty days of the commencement of such procedure (which period may be extended by mutual agreement), or if either party will not participate in a mediation,

[Select one of the following alternatives]

(i) the controversy shall be settled by arbitration in accordance with the Center for Public Resources Rules for Non-Administered Arbitration of Business Disputes, by (a sole arbitrator) (three arbitrators, of whom each party shall appoint one) (three arbitrators, none of whom shall be appointed by either party). (Any mediator or arbitrator not appointed by a party shall be selected from the CPR Panels of Distinguished Neutrals.) The arbitration shall be governed by the United States Arbitration Act, 9 U.S.C § 1-16, and judgment upon the award rendered by the Arbitrator(s) may be entered by any court having jurisdiction thereof. The place of arbitration shall be _____. The arbitrator(s) (are) (are not) empowered to award damages in excess of actual damages, including punitive damages.

(ii) either party may initiate litigation [upon 00 days' written notice to the other party.]

** The Center for Public Resources Model Minitrial Procedure may be substituted for the mediation procedure. 90-120 days would be a reasonable period for this procedure.

Useful Addresses

AAA, 140 West 51st Street, New York, NY 10020-1203, USA. Tel: 212-484 4000

ACAS Headquarters, 27 Wilton Street, London SW1X 7AZ, UK. Tel: 071-210 3000

ADR Net Ltd — *see* IDR (Europe) Ltd

BAE, 90 Bedford Court Mansions, Bedford Avenue, London WC1B 3AE, UK. Tel: 071-637 0333

CAC, University of Kent, Rutherford College, Canterbury, Kent CT2 7NX, UK. Tel: 0227 764000

CEDR, 3-5 Norwich Street, London EC4A 1EJ, UK. Tel: 071-430 1852

CIArb, 24 Angel Gate, London EC1V 2RS, UK. Tel: 071-837 4483

CPR, 366 Madison Avenue, New York, NY 10017, USA. Tel: 212-949 6490

FIRM, 19 London Road, Beaconsfield, Buckinghamshire, HP9 2HN, UK. Tel: (0494) 671177

FMA, The Old House, Rectory Gardens, Henbury, Bristol BS10 7AQ, UK. Tel: (0272) 500140

IDR (Europe) Ltd, Law and Equity Building, 36-38 Baldwin Street, Bristol BS1 1NR, UK. Tel: (0272) 252090; *and* Three Quays, Tower Hill, London EC3R 6DS, UK. Tel: 071-929 1790

LEADR, c/o Level 7, AMP Centre, 50 Bridge Street, Sydney, NSW 2000, Australia. Tel: 02-250 3952

NFCC, Shaftesbury Centre, Percy Street, Swindon, Wiltshire, SN2 2AZ, UK. Tel: (0793) 514055

SPIDR, Suite 512, 1730 Rhode Island Avenue NW, Washington DC 20036, USA

USA&M, 83 South King Street, Suite 806, Seattle, WA 98104, USA. Tel: 206-467 0794

Index